10·18·01

to Cheryl & Basil:

Long time friends & respected collegues:

Fondest regards,

Don + Bob

Werner Blaser

POWELL / KLEINSCHMIDT
INTERIOR ARCHITECTURE

Birkhäuser – Publishers for Architecture
Basel • Boston • Berlin

The essay "Puritan Style" by Werner Blaser was translated from German
into English by Felicity Gloth, Berlin.

A CIP catalogue record for this book is available from the Library of
Congress, Washington D.C., USA.

Deutsche Bibliothek Cataloging-in-Publication Data

Powell, Kleinschmidt: interior architecture / Werner Blaser.
Vorw. Stanley Abercrombie. – Basel ; Boston ; Berlin : Birkhäuser, 2001
ISBN 3-7643-6561-7

Powell/Kleinschmidt
645 North Michigan Avenue
Suite 810
Chicago, IL, 60611 USA
312 642 6450
312 642 5135 Fax

© 2001 Birkhäuser – Publishers for Architecture,
P.O. Box 133, CH-4010 Basel, Switzerland.
http://www.birkhauser.ch
Member of the BertelsmannSpringer Publishing Group

Layout: Werner Blaser, Basel
Litho and typography: Photolitho Sturm AG, Muttenz
Printed on acid-free paper produced from chlorine-free pulp. TCF ∞
Printed in Germany
ISBN 3-7643-6561-7

9 8 7 6 5 4 3 2 1

Contents

Donald D. Powell

After receiving his university degree in architecture and serving as an officer in the United States Air Force Research and Development Command, followed by a Fulbright Traveling Fellowship in Europe, Donald D. Powell joined the Chicago office of Skidmore, Owings & Merrill. He spent 15 glorious years working with the many luminaries in the SOM Chicago office during the Golden Age of that firm. In 1976 he established Powell/ Kleinschmidt, with Robert D. Kleinschmidt based in Chicago.

Robert D. Kleinschmidt

He received his baccalaureate degree in architecture from the University of Illinois, followed by a graduate degree in architecture and landscape design from Columbia University. A William Kinney Fellows Traveling Fellowship provided for a year's study abroad, after which he joined the Chicago office of Skidmore, Owings & Merrill, in 1964. In 1976, along with fellow associate partner Donald D. Powell, he left SOM to establish the firm of Powell/Kleinschmidt, Inc, based in Chicago and specializing in interior architecture and space planning.

Powell/Kleinschmidt
115 South LaSalle Street Office
Chicago, 1976

These offices for interior architecture practice are the embodiment of orderliness and openness; they combine a utilitarianism of purpose with a gracefulness of plan and design. The glass light at the front door, flanked by seasonal flowering plants, invites the visitor and client in.

Materials and fabrics were chosen to provide a neutral background in order that color may come from the architects' work projects. Walls upholstered in Limousine cloth, a wool flannel, are tackable to facilitate study and display of current work in progress.

Six-foot-high English brown oak storage units, 25 feet in length, divide the office's executive-administrative space from the drafting room. The reception area functions as a holding space for clients and manufacturers' representatives, office manager space, and coat storage. With tackable walls for drawings and presentations, the conference area may also be used for slide programs, while the partners' area, with a contemporary version of a traditional partners' desk, affords private space for confidential exchange.

A color and materials laboratory is equipped with storage space and a variety of lighting types for choosing samples.

The drafting room, a model of functional design, has twelve custom-built workstations. Leather-tufted cushions on the window seats provide for rest space, catalogue viewing, or informal conference with a colleague. Files and library material are built into the workstations. The drafting table surfaces are plastic laminate for ease of maintenance. All components combine to make for efficiency and professionalism of the highest order.

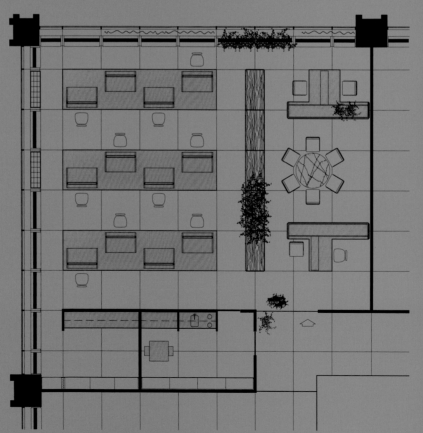

Introduction
by Stanley Abercrombie

The quarter-century of work by Powell/Kleinschmidt summarized in this book is a bridge – a graceful, sound, well-engineered bridge – from the principles of early modernism to the possibilities of future modernism. It sails serenely above the tangle of detours, dead ends, and wrong turns that have misled so many talents less sure of their direction.

Its foundation is in the work of Ludwig Mies van der Rohe. This is not surprising for a firm founded in Chicago, where Miesian influence is still palpable, by two young architects who served their apprenticeships at Skidmore, Owings & Merrill, where Miesian ideals were once revered.

Although Mies is the most obvious progenitor of the P/K style, Powell and Kleinschmidt respect as their models a number of younger talents, prominent among them Davis Allen, Walter Netsch, Bruce Graham, and Jack Dunbar from SOM, Florence Knoll, and Ben Baldwin. They credit another older Chicago master as well, Frank Lloyd Wright. The work of Wright, Robert Kleinschmidt points out, taught them that "the architect can – and should – do everything." Wright's concerns, he and Donald Powell explain, began with the broadest issues of environment and landscape, continued through architecture and interiors, and extended to furniture and the most intimate of accessories. So do theirs. While their practice is limited to interiors and their components, that work is never unrelated to the character of its context, either architectural or natural.

The law offices of Mayer, Brown & Platt, for example, acknowledge their location in the steeply gabled attic of a John Burgee/Philip Johnson postmodern pastiche, a country club dining room (not included here) similarly nods to its architecture's Arts & Crafts origin, and a large accounting firm in the southwest reflects the region's sunlight, space, and warm hues. And, in many cases, the base building materials are the foundation for the creation of an interior materials palette. In all these cases, however, the design manages to be both recognizably appropriate to its setting and recognizably the work of P/K.

What is that recognizable quality? What principles have Powell and Kleinschmidt adopted from the examples of Mies and Davis Allen? What have they rejected from the work of other predecessors and contemporaries? What is the essence of their design? In a word, it is clarity. The clarity of P/K design begins chiefly with the floor plan, and the clarity of the floor plan is necessarily dependent on the forging of an intelligent and functional program of user requirements, which the plan must reflect. At its frequent best, this reflection is quite literal: By looking at – or moving through – a P/K plan, one sees the functional organization, the sense of the firm or organization or family for which it was intended.

The plan also establishes expectations for its own details, its own expression in workstations, seating groups, lighting effects, and materials. Clarity extends to this realm as well. Yet clarity in the work of P/K, if not in the work of some other minimalists, does not mean vacuity. The firm's interiors are simple but never bland, reductionist but never empty, restrained but never boring. P/K design is, in fact, astonishingly alive, vibrant with flashes of color, intelligence, and wit, and informed by a passionate interest in materials, their shadings, textures, and natural character, their scientific properties, and their psychological connotations. There is no surface in any P/K design that has not had the benefit of careful design attention. And some of this attention has been in the form of extensive research projects. For over 30 years, for example, both at SOM and on their own, these two designers have been constantly modifying their specifications for a heavily textured plaster wall treatment; perhaps some day soon they will consider their plaster perfected; perhaps not.

Here, again, the benign spirit of Mies can be felt. For all their obeisance to the rigors of structure, Mies's buildings and interiors often indulged in the pleasures of sensuous materials and finishes – floors of travertine, walls

10

of onyx and primavera, hangings of lemon-yellow silk, hardware of bronze, furniture of steel and leather. Powell and Kleinschmidt work comfortably with such a rich palette, but they have supplemented it with equally interesting and more modestly priced materials – fiberglass screens, straw cloth, nylon-coated lever handles, custom carpet at seven dollars a square yard. Not only price, but also practical considerations of foot traffic, fireproofing, energy conservation, and soil prevention are factored into their design decisions. While P/K interiors are often the site of lavish gestures (the convector covers in their own offices, for example, are of stainless steel), it is more often the case that a striking effect has been achieved by substituting inventiveness for expense. Standard products are often given a fresh slant or an added function (a fabric enlivened with a different yarn color, a side chair transformed into a stacking side chair) by subtle modifications.

Art and plants further enrich P/K interiors. Both Powell and Kleinschmidt are art collectors and connoisseurs; both are passionate and knowledgeable about plant materials, both indoor and out. They manipulate these elements with rare expertise.

And Wright's universal curiosity is felt again in P/K's involvement with the larger issues that lie above and beyond the firm's interiors. The two partners habitually ask the big questions: What should a new office for a lawyer be? What are the necessary components of a modern desk – if, indeed, the desk has not been replaced by the computer? Which elements belong on a module and which do not? What is the proper relationship of executive to clerical work space today? Of public to private residential space? Of city to suburb to country? What is the future nature of business? Of the city? Of the home? These are the generalities that validate the specifics.

The bridge that Powell/Kleinschmidt has built to the future from all these parts is, therefore, an admirable one, but it must be acknowledged that it leads to a particular and limited destination. While P/K's work may at times demonstrate a civil response to postmodernism, it does not lead to further postmodernism. It does not lead to the electronic iconography advocated by Venturi, Scott Brown, nor to the sculptural fantasy practiced by Frank Gehry. And it has nothing in common with the thousand trends and fads that blaze and fade all about us every week. But its focus is its strength. For this prospective traveler into the future, it leads where I would like to go.

Stanley Abercrombie has been editor-in-chief of three design magazines, including, for 14 years, *Interior Design.* He is a Fellow of the American Academy in Rome, a Fellow of the American Institute of Architects, and an Honorary Fellow of the American Society of Interior Designers.

Puritan Style
by Werner Blaser

America's perception of itself as the representative of good taste led to a heightened link between aesthetic and architectural boldness at the time of Thomas Jefferson as far back as the end of the eighteenth century. The concern of art enthusiasts and the president was to refine the taste of their fellow Americans and to obtain the respect and recognition of the world. Consistent use of symmetry was the most conspicuous feature, conveying a great sense of refinement. This instinctive sense of what was right, intended not to be epigonic but original, has been retained and developed until the present day.

Today, America still has pragmatists such as Powell/Kleinschmidt of Chicago, who seek to achieve representation by means of architectural perfection in their interiors. The practical aspects of their interiors lend them special innovative force. They are perfect examples of how handsome and impressive interior architecture emerges from a given building shell, interior architecture which – in an affluent society and with a sense of responsibility arising from dedication – rejects an opulent and ostentatious style. The strictly functionalist impression of the whole is, in other words, especially striking: an almost Puritan style, characterised by resolute, yet extremely sensitive distinctions, is articulated on a qualitatively high level.

It is conceivable that part of the American tradition of modernism understands interior design as being strictly bound by rules: the new design is required to combine functional furniture and art in a given volume. This requires proportions which encompass spaces and concepts that unify, concepts able to keep large volumes small while also capable of shifting the inherent human proportions in the sense of the classical ideals, thereby giving expression to role models and, in consequence, to philosophies of life. These aspirations to synthesize useful and aesthetic aspects are enthusiastic and ambitious, the strategies employed for realisation are innovative: interior design means creating relationships between designed works both architecturally and aesthetically.

In the Tradition of the Pioneers

The principal focus of this interior architecture is on inside space as a conceptual whole. Its art lies in integrating into the work in question the individual as a whole with his methods of thinking and feeling in their spatial sequence.

This book is based on the underlying idea expressed by the formulation "from architecture to furniture": this idea shows that furniture for the interiors of Powell/Kleinschmidt was designed in very close association with specific building tasks. Designing furniture is understood here in a structural context: as construction of the smallest self-contained cell of human living space.

The Chicago virtue is the emotiveness of quality based on its refinement and precision. Minimalist designs of this kind won international recognition and strengthened the self-esteem of the Americans. Mies van der Rohe was the innovator of modern architecture in Chicago. Justly or unjustly, business then appropriated this architecture and won international acclaim. Yet, Mies was, unfortunately, often misunderstood. He cannot be imitated, but his teaching forms the basis for creation of new designs by those who came after him and further development of his principles. Mies van der Rohe's interiors emphasize representation; the same is true of his furniture designs. In the case of these structures and furniture, proportion forms the basis of beauty and harmony, in other words, the individual is the measure of all things.

Apart from Mies van der Rohe, the major pioneers of modern spatial design include Frank Lloyd Wright and Le Corbusier. These ingenious architects created timeless interiors, still valid today, as their clarity, simplicity and choice of exquisite materials evoke the highest degree of spatial effect. Quality of design articulates a clear artistic statement reflected in both interior space and in the furniture.

What these exemplary pioneers have taught us is that the precision and elegance of these interiors led to a new "modern" clarity. Their creations are still today prime examples of aesthetic and technical organisation of the highest order. Yet, what we need today is not "new" interiors, but better ones.

Spatial Composition

Every interior has a core, an innermost principle upon which its design is built. This expressive force generates a strong inner feeling. The subordinate furnishing elements derive their effect from the spatial ensemble. The Chicago architects Powell/Kleinschmidt "diagnosed" their interiors with a specific focus on timelessness and imaginativeness. The underlying structure is oriented to order, dimensions, proportion, materials, surfaces, colors and their balance, design is based on the harmony of visual and haptic qualities. The sequence of modular elements generates internal dynamism; the color scheme and formal language heighten the sense of livability and dignity. By combining content and aesthetic qualities, the strict unity and harmony of the space is symbolised in the form of architecture and furniture.

The furniture elements that have been added to the built spatial volume shape the essence of a clear and logical design, careful in its articulation and thereby readable. The entire spectrum of technical and design aspects dominates interior space as an integrated whole. This calls for architects able to plan such an interior in accordance with the objective criteria that have been described. The test of a spatial composition is its clarity of expression and perception of the whole. These underlying principles are at the root of true spatial design.

The common interest of the two architects is a fundamental study of the concept of space, of the contemporary possibilities of comprehending space and translating these into aesthetic functions. The visual language of interior space makes reference to contrasts and movement, to the use of light and textures. The designed object evokes aesthetic realizations and ways of seeing, even emotion, and we are able to understand what is true, what is valid and what can endure: "Space – it is not emptiness, it is tranquillity and God is in this tranquillity" (Romano Guardini).

The Need to Say Thank-you

The phenomenon of interior architecture leaves many unanswered questions, for example the question of achieving balance between openness and unity. A close look reveals that interiors have become an increasingly meaningful form of design over the last few decades. The work of Donald Powell and Robert Kleinschmidt over the past 25 years reflects the general trend towards creating interiors as an expression of urbanity which is increasingly turning inward; 43 selected projects are presented here. The two architects also pay attention to inconspicuous things in their endeavours, to achieving balance between attention to detail and choice of materials.

In this way, interiors have been elevated to a masterly level: the work of the architects portrayed does not only reveal their close relationship to their master Mies van der Rohe. Each of them has his residence in Chicago in one of the legendary high-rise residential buildings designed by Mies van der Rohe on Lake Michigan, namely at 860 and 880 Lake Shore Drive Apartments respectively. Their walk to their offices on North Michigan Avenue takes them past the former apartment of Mies on East Pearson Street, now called Mies van der Rohe Way.

This book is an opportunity to present the diversity which interior art aspires to achieve today. One aim is to put professional life into a modern context, in other words to develop the world of work into a place where self-perception is appreciated and can evolve newly: beauty that gives the whole its inner necessity. This interior architecture reveals a noblesse of humanity and passionate dynamism, attributes possessed by these two talented architects and their excellent team at their Chicago office. Sincere thanks are due to them all: for their adherence to the Miesian principles of "open" interior spaces and reduction to the Essential.

The Van Meter Residence
Springfield, Illinois, 1976

This schema of refurbishment is an example of a residence that has been redesigned to reflect more adequately the uses and tastes of a growing, maturing family. Cognizance was taken of the exterior pavilion quality, and interiors were planned and directed outward toward an extensive handsomely landscaped property.

The color scheme was derived from the exterior tones of terra-cotta brick and mustard-putty-colored mortar as filtered onto the interior teak paneling of the living room fireplace wall. Interior spaces and furnishings appear in variations of this established palette.

The long lines of the living room were modified by rearrangement of the furnishings into a variety of seating groups. The large U-shaped sofa unit focuses toward the fireplace, while an existing card table was refinished to match a group of classic Wegner chairs upholstered in natural horsehair. Fiberglas insulation was installed on the dining room walls to make the space acoustically more intimate, after which the walls were stretch-upholstered in natural beige linen coordinated with matching table linens.

Stripped of the family's customary accumulative possessions, the guest room was transformed into a refuge for writing projects, sleeping and storage space for luggage. The master bedroom, appointed with seasonal changes of spreads, bolsters and pillows, continues to serve as a favored spot for the family to recapitulate the day's events. In the library there are two desks for the parents, relaxed and orderly space for reading, listening to music, or quiet reflection. The owners' fourteen-year-old daughter, who was born the year her parents moved into their home, was closely involved in the updating of her own bedroom.

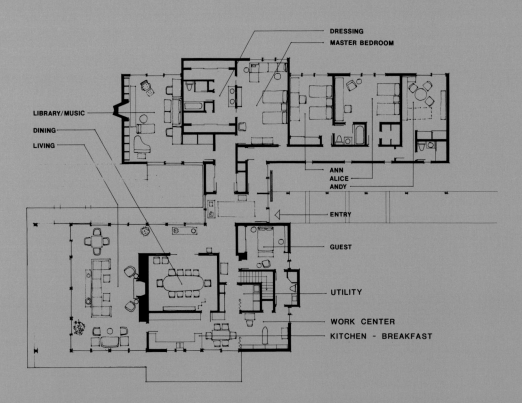

**Gretchen Bellinger Inc. Showroom,
New York, 1979**

"A low-keyed backdrop for the drama of the fabrics." This was the goal of the firm's owner. To open the narrow dimension of the showroom's rectangular shape while simultaneously supplying light to a windowless room, storage cabinets on the lengthwise walls were covered with sliding glass mirrors. The fabrics, all woven natural fibers, are displayed on custom designed rollers of stainless steel, placed on the diagonal and repeating the diagonal pattern of the travertine marble floor and placement of display furniture.
The firm's mushroom-colored Limousine cloth covers the ceiling panels and is also wrapped around the desks, chairs, desk accessories, and notebooks. Incandescent track-lighting fixtures illuminate the fabric displays, offer flexibility, and give true color values.
The firm also represents Saridis Furniture, adapted from designs of the classical Grecian age by T. H. Robsjohn-Gibbings. In addition, pillows and hangings woven by Kenneth Weaver, and one-of-a-kind silk pillows hand-painted by Mia Kodani and Dabi can be seen on display shelves at the end of the showroom. A semi-private area behind the display case accommodates two spaces: the executive office and a secretarial workroom.

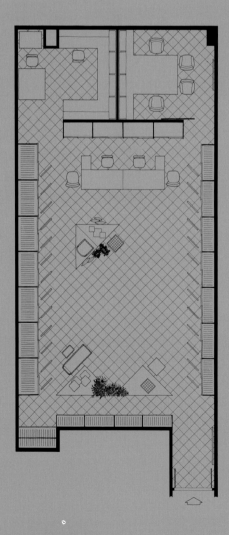

The Kenneth Bellinger Residence
St. Simon's Island, Georgia, 1977

This vacation winter home was conceived, planned, and designed in stark contrast to the owners' principal New England residence. The purpose was to create an alternate life style of quality with the goal of simplicity and ease of maintenance. The plan of containment afforded privacy and security as well as outside gardens and an inside drive, and parking for automobiles and the owners' boat. The existing towering live oak trees are the singular humanizing element of an otherwise flat landscape, distinguishing this home and site from those of its neighbors.

The walled-in living spaces use stucco combined with crushed oyster shells for color and texture, giving a sense of regionalism sympathetic to the locale. The color and materials program, recalling the spirit of the South, was based on judicious use of cotton fabrics, natural wicker furniture and sisal carpets.

Walking through the house, one is struck by the generous amount of space devoted to the kitchen, dining room, and wine storage. This reveals the owners' joy in food preparation for the entertainment of friends and clients. The combination study/office was incorporated into the plan in order that the owner could carry on his business activities.

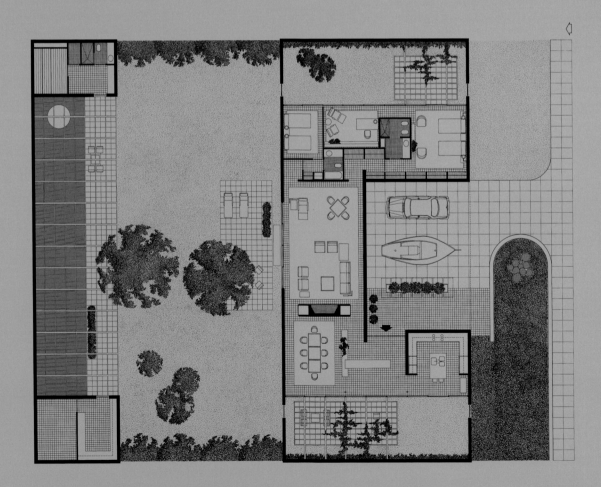

The Prudential Insurance Company of America
Merrillville, Indiana, 1978

Wanting to be assured of a reliable quality work force, The Prudential Insurance Company of America decided to build one of its key satellite facilities in Merrillville, Indiana. A company-ordered survey had confirmed this sought-for benefit.

The structure, designed for 1,150 employees, is built on the open office concept. The building materials consist of precast concrete in tones of beige and black slate flooring, white plaster walls and ceilings, and metal surfaces of stainless steel, complemented by intense shades of red, yellow, blue, and green, all set against a background of flannel gray carpet and lighter toned workstations.

Entrance to the Prudential Merrillville offices is gained via a bridge through a three-story greenhouse after which the visitor comes to the main reception area. Here the focal point is a specially commissioned black and white painting by the artist Al Held; the intersecting and overlapping of geometric forms suggest depth and space.

For a maximum of flexibility, the concept of open office planning was adopted, while offices and conference rooms were clustered around service cores, relating to function of operation in a three-part hierarchy of: circulation area, clerical staff and managerial staff. In order to keep vistas free, no offices were built along the exterior, rather, all are interior.

On the first floor, workstations for four staff members form an H cluster; 42-inch-high panels assure that vision is unimpaired and at the same time provide tack surface plus screening for paperwork organizers. Floors are covered with carpet tiles. Large masses of green plants help to break the rigidity of the workstation pattern.

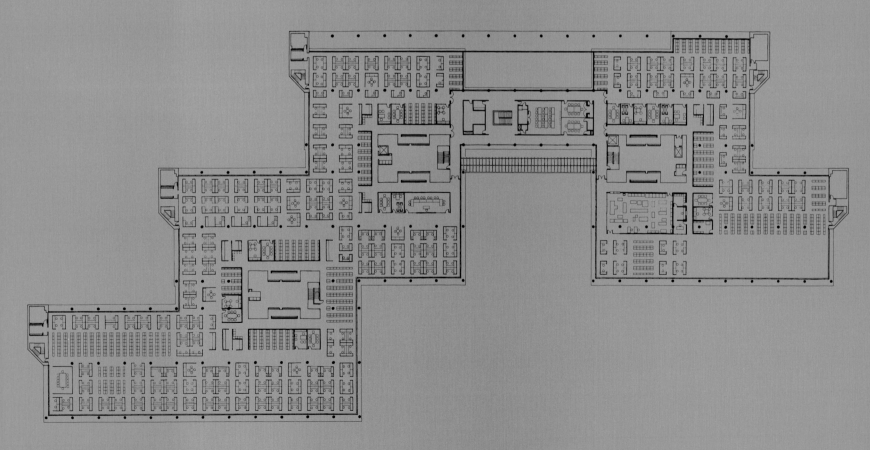

A free-standing wall of frameless glass, darkly tinted, separates the reception area from the third-floor executive area. Ultramarine blue wool jacquard, woven with the Company's Rock of Gilbralter logo, was designed for the reception wall panels. This same fabric is repeated in the bright thematic colors in the interior offices and conference room.

A regional art program was employed for the principal offices and conference rooms, with each occupant and department selecting their own art work. For the public spaces several large paintings, tapestries, and sculptures were commissioned by artists of established reputation. To reduce the length of corridors, a consequence of the arrangement of offices, and to interrupt the monotony of line, neon light sculptures by the artist Chryssa were mounted in tinted plexiglas boxes, allowing the shapes to be reflected in double and multiple images.

Located above the lobby entrance, the main seminar room is equipped with projection facilities and can be subdivided by means of retractable white oak panel walls into three smaller rooms.

In summary, the overriding concern and challenge of the architectural design was to create an environment for the entire company staff that would be pleasing and workable, one in which each employee would feel a productive and significant member of the Prudential organization.

Knoll International Knoll International Knoll International Knoll International Knoll International Knoll International Knoll International Knoll International Knoll International Knoll International Knoll International Knoll In

Knoll International Inc. Showroom,
Chicago, 1978

This project of refurbishment, accomplished in three weeks, was conceived as a restoration. A showroom of former classic qualities had become marred and tarnished as a result of constant commercial promotion and trade shows. The client wanted to reestablish and reinforce the design principles of the founder, Florence Knoll. By opening up a light court that had been covered over for many years, the showroom was transformed by qualities of natural light and sunshine. True color values are now revealed with clarity. Working under the parameter of a limited budget, existing showroom furniture samples were rearranged into appropriate groupings. The firm's own fabrics were utilized for draperies and sliding panels in the light court, and a program for art work, accessories, plants and flowers were also adopted. In consequence, well-designed furniture received display commensurate with its quality.

Study models

CHICAGO MERCANTILE EXCHANGE EXECUTIVE FLOOR

MAYER, BROWN & PLATT TYPICAL RECEPTION ROOM

MAYER, BROWN & PLATT 1/4 FLOOR W/MIRRORS TYPICAL FLOOR

IIT KENT COLLEGE OF LAW LIBRARY, MAIN READING ROOM

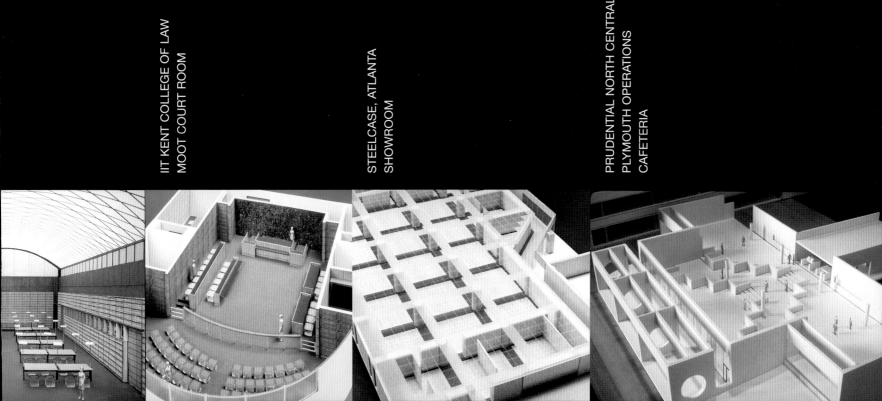

IIT KENT COLLEGE OF LAW
MOOT COURT ROOM

STEELCASE, ATLANTA
SHOWROOM

PRUDENTIAL NORTH CENTRAL
PLYMOUTH OPERATIONS
CAFETERIA

The Vanderbilt Gulfside Apartment
Naples, Florida, 1980

This Florida apartment overlooking the Gulf of Mexico is designed to respond to a congenial and leisurely tropical setting. A less formal way of life is expressed through the furnishings and materials, the consequence of thoughtful attention to the underlying spatial concepts. As the floor plan below illustrates, the space is divided into zones of use: entry, kitchen and food preparation, dining, and living room. On either side space is allocated to quiet and passive uses: rest, sleep, and study. Parallel to the entire apartment is the screened lanai for relaxation and outdoor dining.

Although the building is new, some structural modifications were necessary to impose better organization and balance to the space. By removing a center column and replacing it with a full wall of sliding glass doors, the living room expands completely out onto the lanai, thus capturing a full view of the Gulf. Rearrangement of the kitchen space and walls brought a more functional, symmetrical and spatially richer plan.

Ease of maintenance, an indispensable ingredient for a leisure home, is evident in all the furnishings and materials. Plastic laminate is used in cabinets in the kitchen, both inside and out, and in the living room, bedroom and bath cabinetwork. In order to prevent mildew, cotton fabrics were specified for upholstery, table linens, beds, and baths.

As a corollary to ease of maintenance is the importance of expressing an unmistakable sense of regionalism. In the coloration relating to the shades and tones of the Gulf beach sand, in the use of wicker furniture, and straw cloth panels, and in the art program that echoes the theme of regionalism, this tropical apartment is planned to allow the sea, sky, and shore to cast their spell.

32

One Magnificent Mile Apartment
Chicago, 1982

This apartment is the home of a couple who share an impassioned interest in Greek and Roman antique art and who sought an elegant setting for their collection of artifacts as well as their twentieth century works of art. The owners' complementary enthusiasms are for reading, for cooking, and for entertaining, usually small dinner parties for four.

In responding to the clients' appreciation for visual order, the design is premised on the need for clean lines, simplicity in organization, and an absence of clutter. A sense of regionalism is expressed by color tonalities that relate to the beach sand of Lake Michigan, the water, and the ever-changing skies. Natural materials and fibers used throughout the furnishings, include unfilled travertine floors throughout much of the apartment and natural wool carpets in the library, corridor, master bedroom, and an area rug in the living room. To maximize the use of space, built-in perimeter seating faces in toward the rooms and out to the spectacular view of the lake.

From the octagonally-shaped foyer, the gallery leads to the living room, whereas a corridor leads to the library and master bedroom. The living room contains prized Greek chairs, designed by T. H. Robsjohn-Gibbings and manufactured by Saridis of Athens. The sofa is upholstered in natural Moroccan fabric custom hand-woven for this project, and the square bronze mirror-polished coffee table with a gallery edge acts as a piece of sculpture. Sand-colored leather wall panels mark the termination and focal point for the end of the living room.

The marble dining room table with its circular top and cone-shaped base was custom-designed by Powell/Kleinschmidt as was a special wall-hung buffet, wrapped in leather with a honed-finished travertine top, that gives the wall a sculptural look.

For inspiration, the architects turned to the design of the structure so that the geometry of the building is reflected in the travertine and carpet patterns, ceiling domes, and lights. The master bedroom continues the design of expanding space through careful orchestration of the color tonalities of all surfaces as well as the scale and detail of each furniture component.

Throughout the apartment, quiet grandeur is the theme as all the spaces encourage philosophical and artistic meditation.

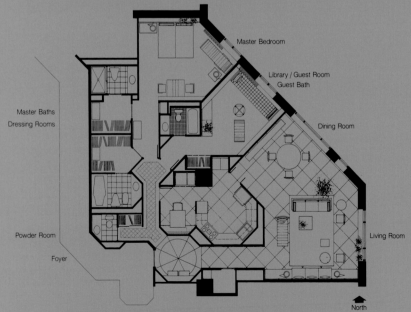

Master Bedroom

Library / Guest Room
Guest Bath

Master Baths
Dressing Rooms

Dining Room

Powder Room

Living Room

Foyer

North

The Prudential Insurance Company of America

North Central Plymouth Operations, Plymouth, Minnesota, 1981

Built into the side of a hill near a lake, this four-story structure, designed to accommodate a maximum of 1,900 employees, responds to the need for energy conservation. With the earth acting as a natural insulator, the northern elevation is two stories and the southern elevation is four. On the north, less surface area is exposed to the harsh winter winds, and the south fenestration permits the sun to enter in a controlled fashion.

During the programming phase, Powell/Kleinschmidt conducted interviews with 300 employees to elicit information regarding workstation requirements, work relationships, adjacencies, storage needs, and other vital data. Based on these responses, workstation types were devised that respond to the building module and are carefully coordinated with the underfloor power and telephone systems. The workstations take into account the working characteristics of the employees, the requisite degree of mobility, and the size of various working divisions. Pleasing offices with large glazed areas overlook the general work areas. The unique office shapes permit oblique observation of employees and at the same time offer privacy to the occupant.

The color and material palette reflects the subdued spectrum of the Minnesota setting and the regional Nordic influence. The colors are compatible with each other and therefore permit interchange.

Included in the project was an art program in which the artists were drawn from the North Central region of the country. More than 300 works of art representing 120 artists were purchased by the client. In the spirit of good neighbors and justifiable corporate pride, the client offers tours of the building to interested residents and visitors.

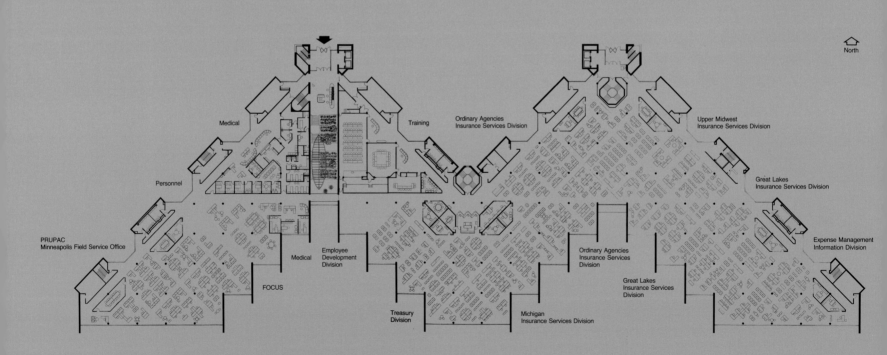

Northwestern University School of Law
Chicago, 1984

This structure is an elegant addition to the older law school building, a 1920 work by James Gamble Rodgers. The project represents the strong collaboration between the architectural firm of Holabird & Root, the Building Committee of the School of Law, and the interior architectural firm of Powell/Kleinschmidt. From the outset of space planning and programming through construction and final occupancy, this collaborative effort responded to all the project's requirements for classrooms, auditorium, moot court, library, faculty offices, student studies, and lounge areas.

Three different designs were employed for the three large classrooms. One classroom is provided with unpadded wooden seats, similar to those of the older law school building and reminiscent of an earlier age of legal training. The second has the luxury of upholstery, while the third is laid out as a mock courtroom to evoke an air of authenticity. In all, theatre-like changes of level assure effective rapport between lecturer and audience. The spaces, festively launched, have added to the esteem of the School of Law and to the enhancement of daily life for faculty and students alike.

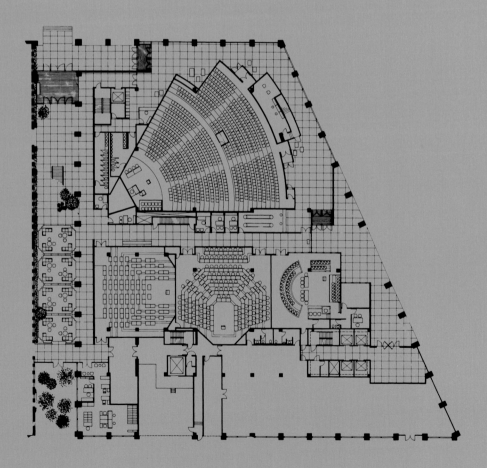

860 Lake Shore Drive Apartment
Chicago, 1985

In Mies van der Rohe's celebrated steel-and-glass tower at 860 Lake Shore Drive, Chicago, this 1,700-square-foot apartment was thoroughly remodeled by Powell/Kleinschmidt for partner Donald Powell's own use. Its conventional three-bedroom layout was replaced by a much more open plan, its flow of space modulated by a free-standing T-shaped storage unit. The unit, however, is raised slightly above the floor and stops well short of the ceiling, furthering the open effect. The apartment is furnished with both Miesian designs, such as the dining chairs, these last specially commissioned by the architects working with Mies' original drawings. Interior finishes include travertine flooring, teak paneling, and wall coverings woven of steel mesh, and upholstery in wool and leather. Colors are muted throughout, with visual focus on a changing display of art and on the views of Lake Michigan and Chicago's Gold Coast.

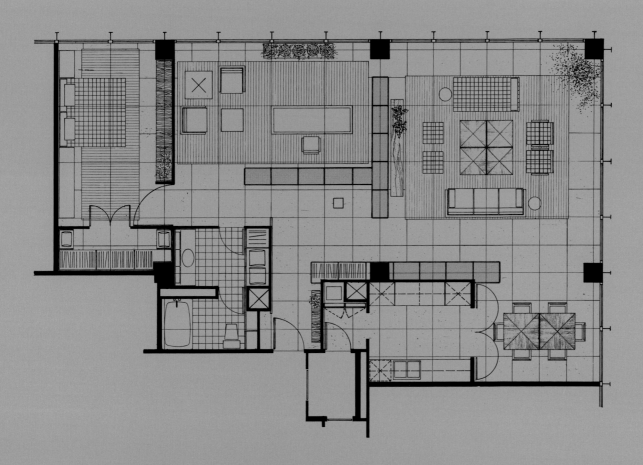

Steelcase/Stow & Davis Showroom,
Atlanta, Georgia, 1985

This 17,500-square-foot showroom was designed for the display of two furniture companies' products: Steelcase and Stow & Davis. The underlying design principle of this new showroom in the Atlanta Market Center was to create architectonic enclosures that would demonstrate the distinctive features of the furniture systems and their application to today's market. The emphasis was on the exhibition of the products in a space conducive to their comprehension and potential sale.

The entrance to the showroom was designed as a grand gesture with a feeling of splendor. It consists of two bays, void of furniture as in a classical manner, permitting guests to congregate.

A large presentation room, with a movable wall which divides the space into two rooms, is equipped for a media presentation as an introduction to the furniture systems on display.

The exhibit space consists of the three bay by three bay, a classic tectonic grid, in which the columns serve as the principal spatial element. The floor space consists of nine bays, with each bay outlined in granite and carpet insets to reemphasize the architectural pattern. The ceiling similarly echoes the grid pattern of the floor. Those portions of the ceiling between the columns are lowered to enclose the HVAC system and simultaneously give structure and modulation to the space while making distances comprehensible. Because the columns were of differing size, a decision was made to wrap them so as to make them uniform, thus softening the lines and, at the same time, bringing in conduits and power lines. Within this design, the products are kept distinct. However, an overall view permits one to see the escalating hierarchies of the two furniture lines.

In the staff area, the furniture systems are grouped in workstation configurations so that a client can visualize how the display would appear in his or her office environment. At the far end of the showroom is an extension of space that accommodates both open and private offices.

To create an illusion of space along the windowless exterior, steel window walls were installed, painted black, and the panels filled with white sandblasted glass, lit from behind. The effect is to make the space more humane, bright, and welcoming.

The materials used for the showroom were chosen for their regional qualities. The floors are Southeast domestic marble and granite, and the column covers are finished to match Georgia pecan wood. The walls are painted off-white, and the steel window wall units that repeat the exterior walls are painted black with glass panels; together, the materials provide a quiet backdrop for the drama of the furniture.

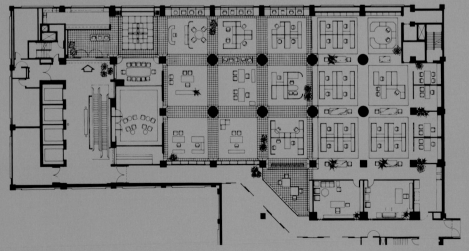

Powell/Kleinschmidt Office
645 North Michigan Avenue, Chicago, 1986

In their previous office having learned what space allocations worked most successfully and which areas required adjustment or refinement, the partners of this interior architectural firm planned their new and enlarged offices in such a way as to capitalize on their earlier experience.

The concept of an open drafting room, which permitted visual and verbal communication between the design and production sectors, was retained. The daily interaction that allowed each professional staff member to see what other colleagues were engaged in and how projects were developing was of inestimable value. The areas requiring additional space involved service functions such as record and project files, doubling of the Colors & Materials Laboratory, greater and more efficient display space for client review. The new accountant position necessitated a totally separate workstation. Two new spaces were developed for marketing and business development activity and for related special projects.

The reception/waiting area was designed to give the firm's receptionist strategic visual control of all staff activities as well as greeting clients, sales representatives, and other guests. The gallery contiguous to the reception area contains coat storage, a conference alcove where staff members can meet with sales representatives, and a raised platform for model display.

On one side of the gallery area there is a large conference room for client presentations and meetings. It includes a drop-down screen and slide projector for review of past work plus display areas for drawings, plans, and renderings. Beyond, the partners' area offers complete privacy for conversation, discussion, and telephone calls, in addition to the genuine need for retreat from daily drafting room activity. On the opposite side of the gallery are found a print room, which accommodates a CADD plotter, a drawing printer, and storage for office and art supplies, plus a designated area for the copy machine and a compact office pantry.

The brightest areas of the new space along the two window walls are assigned to the drafting room personnel, giving a sense of both inner space and space beyond the building. In the areas farthest from the windows, special controlled lighting was designed and installed, appropriate to the specific function of each area. During the past 15 years since the space was initially completed and photographed, each workstation has been equipped with a computer and computer aided drafting.

The salutary effect of the enlarged spaces has been manifested in the espirit de corps and increased productivity. It has also reaffirmed the principle of designing environments for working and living that are effective, responsive to the client's needs, welcoming and humane.

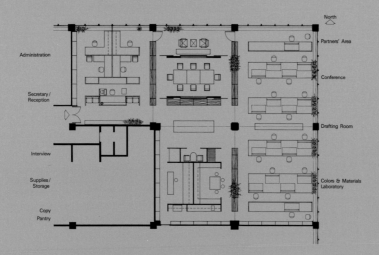

Chicago Mercantile Exchange Executive Office
Chicago, 1987

As corporate and business enterprises expand, so does the need for greater effectiveness in the use of space and patterns of circulation. This was the case with the executive offices of the Chicago Mercantile Exchange, which, as the consequence of its meteoric growth, could no longer tolerate the cramped layout and circulation congestion.

In resolving this dual problem, Powell/Kleinschmidt recommended the complete demolition of existing offices and redesigning the entire floor. The new plan separates the formal visitor and reception areas, with access to the boardroom, from the executive offices area. The key to clarifying the circulation problem was the introduction of a 30-foot-long stainless steel bridge, suspended over a large atrium.

Because this floor represents the public face of the Chicago Mercantile Exchange, the client was eager to impart a sense of welcome to the distinguished visitors who come from all countries of the world. The reception desk provides space for two computer screens, two printers, and two people. The height was kept to a minimum so that a sense of welcome rather than preponderance would be imparted to guests. The memorabilia corridor through which guests pass contains artifacts and photographs depicting the history of the Exchange.

The new VIP gallery is fitted with built-in buffet cabinets which are used for receptions and social gatherings. A custom carpet is patterned with the outline of a house, exemplifying this sense of welcome. At the same time, large glass panels afford a dramatic view of the trading floor below. The boardroom, increased in size as a consequence of the new bridge, is now a generous space seating over 30 people at a boat-shaped table. Five suspended clocks indicate the five major international markets. To relate the building's architectural character to the interior spaces, Powell/Kleinschmidt specified materials that refer to the exterior Carnelian granite and a harmonizing color palette of terra cotta and teak. The sawtooth architectural motif is repeated in table legs and other design elements.

The redesigned executive floor now functions consistent with the client's goals and with its role as one of the world's leading commercial exchanges.

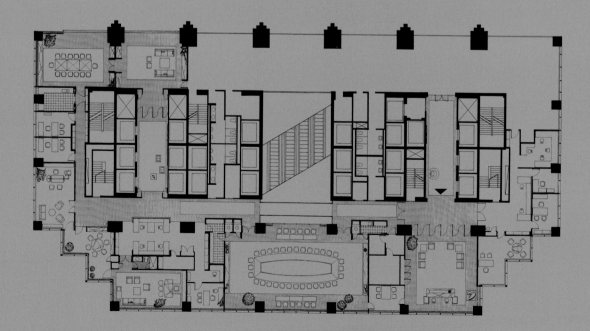

Mayer, Brown & Platt Law Offices,
Chicago, 1988–2001

As much as any other project, the Mayer, Brown & Platt Law Offices epitomize the breadth of interior architectural and space planning services offered by Powell/Kleinschmidt. Mayer, Brown & Platt is one of Chicago's largest and most distinguished law firms. And when its growth dictated a new location, the partnership chose 190 South LaSalle Street as its new site. The building, designed by the Office of John Burgee with Philip Johnson in a postmodern style, attracted wide attention. Occupying the top eleven levels of the new structure originally, the firm has expanded its spaces to include additional floors. Powell/Kleinschmidt continues to assist Mayer, Brown & Platt with these additions, thus providing design continuity.

The relocation from a building with a large floor plate with horizontal patterns of circulation to one less than half the size with the resultant need for vertical patterns of circulation meant considerable restructuring and reorganization. The law firm's Move Committee, with whom Powell/Kleinschmidt worked throughout the project, emphasized the need for adequate elevator capacity and incorporation of other technologies for efficient circulation of books, files, records, and mail. The client was similarly firm in its insistence that the design reflect Mayer, Brown & Platt's long-held tradition of dignity and quiet competence.

Mayer, Brown & Platt, which groups its 490 attorneys and their assistants in an unstructured pattern rather than by specialty, asked that the design be expressive of a high degree of equality and standardization, floor to floor. Conference rooms are concentrated on the 39th level, which also serves as the principal reception floor for most visitors. Secondary reception areas are also found on levels 31, 33, and 36.

The fortieth floor, the uppermost floor of the building, is as unique in its skyline silhouette as it is in its interior design. It houses the law firm's library, a mezzanine-ringed reading room, planned by Powell/Kleinschmidt but designed by Johnson/Burgee. The room is a departure from the law firm's basic design. A Victorian air prevails with cast-iron filigree, figured carpet, and giant chandeliers. The space to the north of the library is used for large staff meetings and as a mock courtroom.

The art program is an amalgam of old and new. All are works on paper. The collection of 18th and 19th century maps of Chicago, the Midwest, the Chicago Rapid Transit system, and railroad posters of the 1920s was inventoried and catalogued. Selected pieces were restored and reframed and hung throughout the typical floors. For the 39th floor and some of the partners' offices, modern works were added. The curator for the entire collection is Frank D. Mayer, a grandson of one of the firm's founders.

The offices have received broad critical acclaim. Highest tribute, however, comes from all the people for whom these new spaces are home.

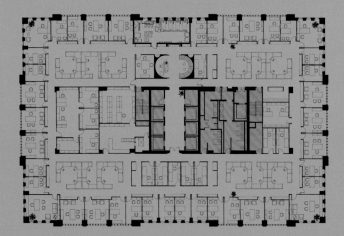

AND ITS MYSTERY
FIELD MUSEUM
Y HE CHICAGO APID RANSIT

880 Lake Shore Drive Apartment
Chicago, 1989

This apartment for P/K principal Robert Kleinschmidt's own use adheres to the principles of its building architecture, designed in 1949 by Ludwig Mies van der Rohe, and it is furnished largely with Mies' own furniture
designs. Two adjacent 880-square-foot apartments were combined into a single unit, one of the former bedrooms being converted into a study area. A sequence of linked spaces unfolds from the entrance through a
music alcove to the corner of the living room with its spectacular Lake Michigan views. An adjacent dining area
is raised two steps for an even better view and is defined by a glass-topped serving counter, its sensuously bio-
morphic outline referring to both an early skyscraper scheme by Mies and the waves lapping the shore below.
Millwork walls and cabinetry are given a hand-rubbed white lacquer finish or are fabric covered, and the flooring is quartered white oak with a dark brown finish. The apartment is an effective stage for Kleinschmidt's con-
tinual rotation of artwork, accessories, fabrics, and seasonal flowers and plants.

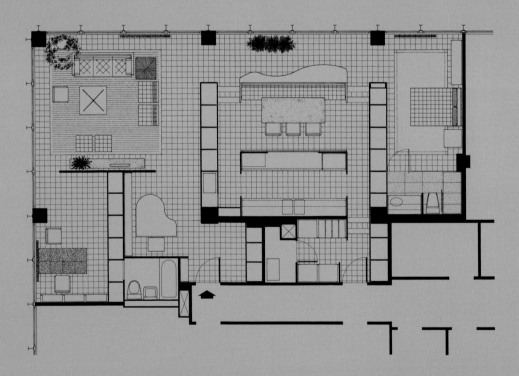

Woodwork Corporation of America
Chicago, 1989

In refurbishing its executive and sales offices, the client, one of the Midwest's finest custom millwork manufacturers, stipulated a design program that would convey a strong sense of craft and the expert capabilities of the
firm, thus creating a showcase for Woodwork Corporation of America to the architectural community.

Powell/Kleinschmidt responded by incorporating into the design program a choice combination of different
woods and finishes, ranging from hand-rubbed lacquer and open-pore lacquer to high-gloss polyester-stained
particle board, and marquetry. A matrix of French white ash paneling and American cherry banding was developed for a spatial and visual distribution of clerestories, materials, open and enclosed spaces. The columns are
clad in high-gloss polyester.

Visitors who are directed to the reception area immediately sense the quality of the company's products. The
built-in seating is integrated into the architecture of the room. The custom-designed coffee table incorporates
sunburst ash veneer with solid cherry and a bullnose edge, while the three pairs of table legs pierce the table
surface and are braced with ash dowels. Together with the harmonizing wood doors, the spaces say "Welcome
to Woodwork Corporation of America."

Warm incandescent ceiling lights complement the tones and textures of the wood. A combination of direct and
indirect lighting occurs in the corridor, whereas indirect lighting is used on top of the cabinets, allowing light to
bounce off the ceiling for additional illumination. Similar care was taken to provide a well-lit background for staff
working at CRT screens.

The company's president arranged his collection of antique tools as a collage on the wall behind his office desk.
An art program was tailored to expand upon the sense of craft with a number of commissioned pieces. Of
immense gratification is the client's pleasure in the refurbished spaces. The highly successful program was similarly praised by guests attending the opening reception and tour.

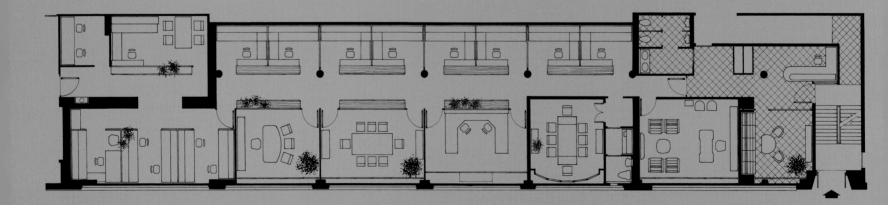

Standard Club of Chicago
Chicago, 1988–1992

As one of the nation's most prestigious private clubs located in a distinguished 1916 Albert Kahn building, the Standard Club of Chicago engaged Powell/Kleinschmidt to initiate a major renovation of six floors in its gathering spaces. This project, phased over several years, has brought the historic club building back to its original luster.

Phase One focused on the main dining room and its foyer as the crown jewel of the Club. Outdated furniture and finishes were replaced, windows were uncovered to allow natural light to filter in, new walnut paneling was designed to match the period style of the building, and the elegant and historic molded plaster ceiling was restored. This room was given dramatic focus by the twenty-eight foot Sol Lewitt mural commissioned for the north wall.

Successive renovations, each reinforcing the Renaissance elegance of the historic 1916 Albert Kahn designed structure, include the ground floor reception lobbies, the ballroom and its ancillary spaces, and twenty-two meeting rooms. The strong collaboration of Powell/Kleinschmidt and this Club continues with each new phase of renovation.

First National Bank of Chicago
Executive Dining 57th Floor, Chicago, 1989

The client, a leading Chicago-based bank that enjoys an international reputation in the world of banking and finance, was eager to refurbish the entire 57th floor executive dining area. The 20-year-old space had been heavily used and, as a consequence, was somewhat threadbare and faded and no longer a source of pride or pleasure. At the same time, the client wanted to ensure that any program of renovation be respectful of the building's architecture and reflective of the bank's role and stature within the financial community.

Three areas of the 57th floor were singled out for total architectural changes to bring them up to the level of design, compatible with the rest of Powell/Kleinschmidt's renovation. The "Backroom," previously divided into three small separate rooms, was restored to a single room. The chairman's dining room was redesigned from a traditional mode to a modern one, giving it a better sense of scale and balance. Finally, the southeast Banquet Room was brought up to the level of the remainder of the floor. An entirely new chair was designed to provide improved seating for the main dining room, a space that accommodates 150 diners. A related goal of the program of refurbishment was to work with the bank's art curator in arranging more advantageous settings for the impressive collection of artwork.

New furniture consisted of seating and tables in the private dining rooms, where new wall-hung credenzas give added storage, improved service, and have alleviated traffic bottlenecks. The new custom wool carpeting is taken from a range of gray hues, the darkest charcoal in the areas of heaviest traffic use and the lightest in less used areas. Nine Louis Sullivan windows, originally designed and installed in a land office in Algona, Iowa, were purchased by the bank, framed in bronze, and mounted in groups of three. Together, they provide accents of color throughout the floor.

A final point of interest is that the complete construction and installation were accomplished within a period of eight and one-half weeks. To inaugurate the new spaces, the bank arranged a series of social events.

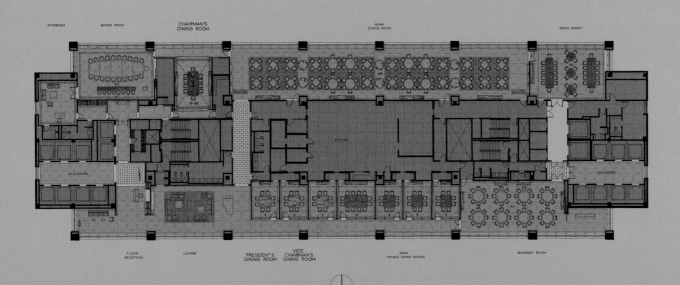

Illinois Institute of Technology
Kent College of Law, Chicago, 1990

Powell/Kleinschmidt's involvement with this project in the earliest stages of design allowed for a strong collaboration with the building architect Holabird & Root. For this reason, programming and interior planning became integral factors in the overall design success of this ten-story building.

Working closely with the faculty and administration committee throughout the project, Powell/Kleinschmidt ensured that all requirements for the most modern education and practice of law were incorporated within this major new facility. Lecture rooms incorporate the most current acoustics, lighting, audiovisual and computer equipment with the flexibility needed to accommodate inevitable advances in technology. The moot courtroom was designed to government standards and has been used for actual criminal trials. Other facilities include a major law library, a 400-seat auditorium, faculty offices, computer research centers, a cafeteria and a variety of lecture facilities. Furnishings and finishes were designed to be attractive, upbeat, easy to maintain, and functional while keeping within the designated budget. The completed design provides a facility unmatched as a precision tool for legal education.

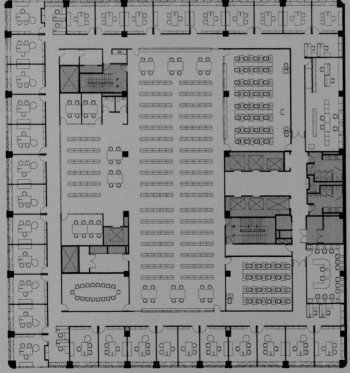

Typical Office/Library Floor

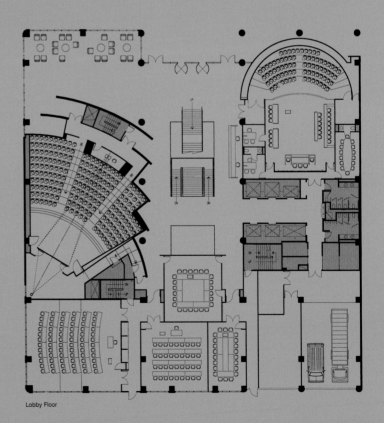

Lobby Floor

SunarHauserman
Furniture Collection, 1988

The basic premise of the lounge seating and tables designed by Robert D. Kleinschmidt for SunarHauserman was to incorporate the principles of ergonomics in lounge seating, and to do it in a way that is classic and timeless. Long-term comfort, modularity of selection, and economy of manufacture are reflected in the entire line of chairs and sofas. The collection consists of three specific series: low arm, wing back and high back series. To complement the seating series, Kleinschmidt also designed two different tables that are offered in a choice of materials and sizes.

Ottoman

Low Back Series

Wing Back Series

High Back Series

Some Possible Configurations

Grippo & Elden Law Offices
Chicago, 1990

The new Grippo & Elden law offices occupy one floor in the recently completed AT&T Corporate Center in Chicago's west loop. Planning of the space was based on the young law firm's strong desire to have all its offices on a single floor of the building. In addition, the client had the following stipulations: (1) that a strict budget be adhered to; (2) that a contemporary design be implemented regardless of the Art Deco character of the building; and (3) that the design accommodate the firm's policy of having legal assistants rather than secretaries maintain the office's files.

To respond to the one-floor instruction, the core element was expanded to include the library, copy center, production center, mail room, legal assistant offices, and other support spaces. This left the perimeter of the floor open for offices, conference rooms, and secretarial stations. Offices for the senior partners are located in the building's four corner spaces, while quadrants of secretarial workstations occupy the four open areas adjacent to the senior partners' offices.

Upon entering the Grippo & Elden law offices, one is greeted by a terrazzo floor with a mosaic pattern related in design to the building's lobby. The colors have been kept to a minimal black, white, and gray palette to display with optimum effect the two opposing wood feature walls of the reception room. The wood accent walls are a matrix of alternating bands of Bubinga and Sapele wood veneers. All patterns generated in the floor and on the walls are based on the building's 5-foot construction module. This rhythmic pattern eventually leads one's eyes to the commanding views of the city from the conference rooms. Light enters the reception area through the white frosted glass walls that provide visual and acoustic privacy in the firm's conference rooms.

At the client's request, a mock-up was made of the custom-designed cluster of secretarial workstations for each quadrant of the floor to make certain it met every requirement for function, storage capacity, and size. Concealed storage for filing, with doors that open on top of each unit, prevent clutter and add to the general appearance of the staff offices.

A final note: Powell/Kleinschmidt undertook an extensive investigation of several Chicago buildings to determine which one best lent itself to Grippo & Elden's programmatic needs. The building recommended to the client met every requirement. Upon occupation of several years, it functions handsomely for lawyers, associates, and staff.

University of Chicago
Graduate School of Business, Chicago, 1991

Powell/Kleinschmidt's careful analysis of project goals based on exchange between client and the building architects Lohan Associates has resulted in the tremendous success of this important addition to Chicago's business
center in this structure on the north bank of the Chicago River.

Consisting of 105,000 square feet, the new facility for the University of Chicago consists of meeting spaces for
use by both University and outside groups. To meet these unique needs, the building was planned with the flexibility to house a multitude of functions from standard lectures and seminars to banquets and large gatherings.
To accomplish this, meeting rooms are equipped with state-of-the-art acoustics, lighting and audio-visual equipment. In addition, many spaces can be reconfigured quickly to house varying sizes or types of meetings. These
spaces are complemented by faculty offices, lounges and a student bookstore to form a full-service education
facility with the flexibility for growth and change required by this forward-thinking institution.

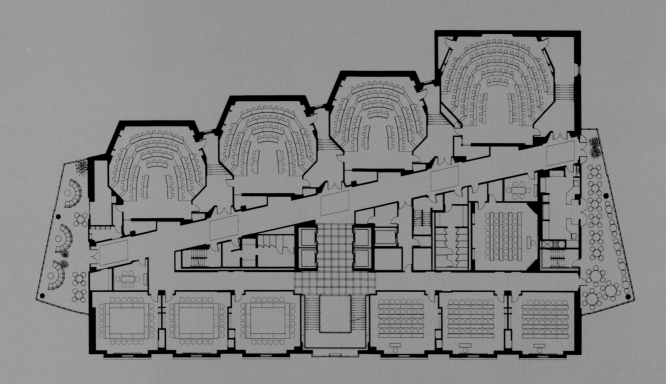

Custom Details

CHICAGO MERCANTILE
EXCHANGE
BOARD ROOM CLOCKS

CHICAGO MERCANTILE EXCHANGE
BASE AND CORNER DETAIL

MAYER, BROWN & PLATT
ENTRY KEY CARD HOLDER

GRETCHEN BELLINGER INC.
FABRIC DISPLAY BELT HOLDER

P/K OFFICE 645 NORTH MICHIGAN
COMPUTER PEDESTAL

P/K OFFICE 645 NORTH MICHIGAN
DOOR PULL

Fruit of the Loom
Corporate Aircraft, 1992

In today's fast-paced world of business, time frequently translates into corporate profits versus corporate losses. To facilitate the decision-making process for corporate executives, companies frequently resort to private aircraft as a means of on-site investigation and discussion of critical issues affecting the company's future. In the case of this corporate client, the chief executive officer directed that the custom-designed interiors of the company's aircraft express a strong contemporary spirit, reflective of our technology-driven economy. The client rejected the heavy walnut paneling of many corporate aircraft in favor of an interior that conveyed a lightness of weight, spacial expansion and color tone, as well as comfort and ease of maintenance throughout the interior. A simple yet conservative palette of colors was selected consisting of shades of gray, black and minimal accents of red and blue to provide a restful backdrop during flight. Seating comfort is assured in chairs with superior support plus upholstery fabric soft in texture. The lighting was fine-tuned to accommodate reading, talking, or the occasional much-needed rest.

The wisdom of the client's instructions is clearly enforced as one views the glistening white exterior of the aircraft, set off by a four-inch stripe of navy blue punctuated by a one-inch overlay band of bright red recalling the runway markings. The aircraft forcefully reflects the company's image in every regard.

GATX Corporation
Corporate Headquarters, Chicago, 1992

The corporate headquarters of GATX, a Fortune 500 company, occupies 175,000 square feet on the top seven floors of 500 West Monroe Street. Open workstations, three basic office sizes, an executive suite, boardroom, conference room, employee cafeteria, and a computer center are included within this project. The goal, articulated unequivocally by the company's chairman, was to create a strong corporate image and highly productive environment within a tight budget and schedule.

Powell/Kleinschmidt has accomplished this goal by creating a sense of community, corporate-wide, while giving separate identity to each division. The seven floors are dramatically linked with an open stair on each floor, creating a unique vertical gathering space for exchange of ideas. Each of the three main corporate divisions is given identity with the use of individual, but complementary, color and material palettes. The executive suite is given special identity with the economical use of anigre veneer and neutral color tones. The boardroom, created within a two-story space, was designed to convey its hierarchical position in the corporate structure without excessive expense or construction delays.

Throughout the entire project, careful consideration was given to the need to be able to adjust to any future reorganization, a requirement typical in today's corporate world, and to do so swiftly, imaginatively, and with a minimum of physical upheaval and work flow interruption.

In summary, every requirement stipulated at the outset of the assignment was fully met. Not only was the project completed and installed on the agreed-upon date; it conformed fully to the project budget.

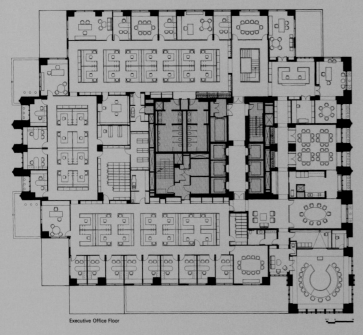

Executive Office Floor

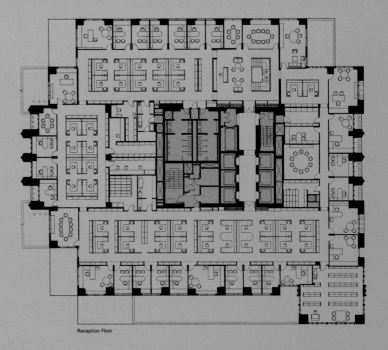

Reception Floor

The Art Institute of Chicago Museum Shop
Chicago, 1993

This completely redesigned and renovated shop provides a vibrant and attractive space for sales while complementing the stately museum building of which it is a part. Accomplished in the face of many hurdles, such as a strict budget, and a greatly accelerated schedule, an additional requirement was to keep the store open during construction.

Offering a wide variety of dynamic product displays, the primary sales gallery forms a transition from museum to shop. Rows of tall display cases march down each side of the room, drawing customers into a grand hall for browsing and shopping. Suspended ceilings were removed to uncover the original 106-year-old plaster ceiling. The added height and meticulously restored ceiling details combine to form a sophisticated and dramatic space. From here, the customer is drawn to various sales spaces and alcoves, each of which is fitted with flexible and interchangeable display cases. These cases integrate lighting, hardware, and electronics to form a unique environment for a diverse and ever-changing product line. The materials palette is derived from the extensive use of limestone as a base building material and flooring. Lacquered casework, walls, and all finishes relate to these color tonalities to create the most neutral background for merchandise displays. Throngs of delighted shoppers bear witness to the effectiveness of the elegantly restored museum shop.

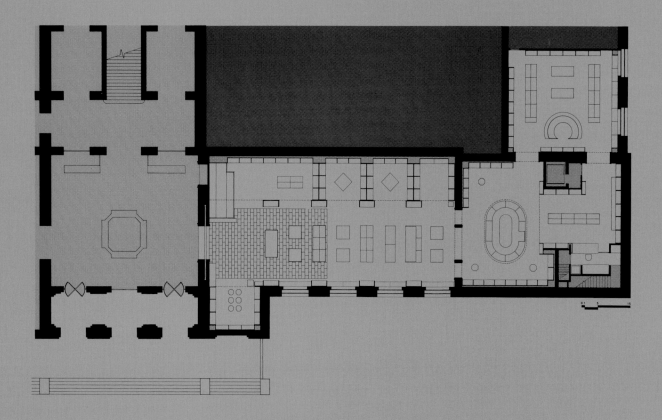

Ryan-Kralovec Penthouse
Chicago, 1992

This project concerned the restoration and renovation of a two-story penthouse located atop the Mies van der Rohe designed "Commonwealth Promenade" apartment tower. The directive from the new owners was to "honor the work of Mies' original plan by returning to the original design concept." The work was based on the original plans and drawings held in the archives of the Chicago Historical Society and the Museum of Modern Art in New York.

The apartment consists of a living room, dining room, and kitchen on the lower level with bedrooms and study on the second level. On the lower level, only the kitchen required major renovation. Original walnut paneling in the dining room was replaced with new walnut paneling, while the gray-veined white marble floor was pulticed and cleaned to its original brightness. An antique Persian rug now forms the basis for the classic Mies furniture and some Powell/Kleinschmidt designed furniture and owner-collected antiques. To take advantage of spectacular nocturnal views, new lighting was designed so that no reflective glare from interior sources of light would interfere with the drama of the city aglow at night. A black silk drapery on the wall of the east window screens the adjacent building and provides material contrast in softness to the hard stone floor. The interior stairwell, consisting of aluminum stringers and risers, white marble treads, and a square, aluminum bar-rail, provides a dramatic element connecting the two levels. An outdoor terrace paved in the same white marble wraps around three sides of the lower floor, offers an outdoor connection and pleasure throughout the season, and, of equal importance, extends the space in the most serene manner. The result is an elegant and graceful residence.

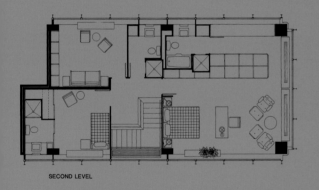

SECOND LEVEL

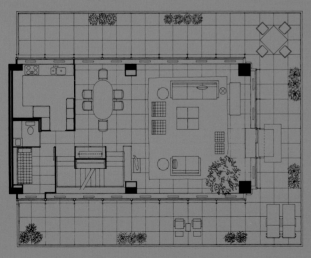

FIRST LEVEL

John D. & Catherine T. MacArthur Foundation
Administrative Offices, Chicago, 1994

The offices of the MacArthur Foundation occupy space in the Marquette Building, a structure listed on the National Register of Historic Places. Because the Foundation represents the loftiest ideals of new world aesthetics, its strong commitment to conservation prohibited the use of any materials on the endangered species list. It also insisted on a modest budget that conserved assets consistent with its nonprofit mission, rejecting any overspending on its own operations.

To honor these commendable virtues, Powell/Kleinschmidt designed desk systems made of compressed particle board, a highly-dense product of wood remnants, rather than rare wood veneers. A careful study was made of lighting requirements throughout all the spaces, culminating in an energy-conscious system that won an award from the International Association of Lighting Designers. Powell/Kleinschmidt, respectful of the historic structure, retained and took advantage of the large "Chicago-style" windows. Perimeter offices and conference rooms benefit from expanded views and higher ceilings, creating a truly unique workspace without depleting financial or natural resources.

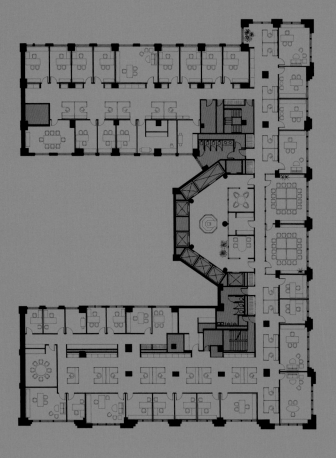

Rooks, Pitts and Poust Law Offices
Chicago, 1994

This prominent Chicago law firm engaged Powell/Kleinschmidt to design an office environment within a limited budget that would convey dignity, and simultaneously provide a comfortable, efficient workplace for staff and clients. This was accomplished by creatively reusing components left by a previous tenant. Existing doors were refinished, abandoned files were reconfigured and repainted, and existing walls and light fixtures were used whenever possible. Upgraded finishes were used sparingly at those locations capable of producing the greatest visual impact. An open stair connects the two floors of this project, providing ease of communication while adding a dramatic focal point to the reception lobby. The building's unusual floor plan, containing three different corner configurations, was a particular challenge. Imaginative planning by Powell/Kleinschmidt maximized the number of perimeter private offices and increased floor plan efficiency.

Powell/Kleinschmidt has given this client a distinctive and highly functional work environment at moderate cost. The value of efficient planning and value-engineered design is now measured in higher staff morale and increased productivity.

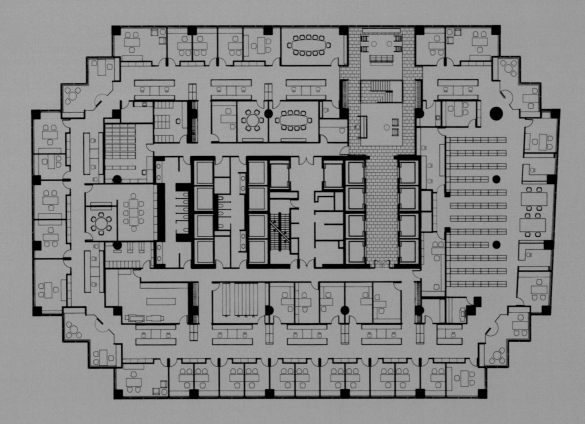

Pickleman Apartment
Chicago, 1994

This apartment, a combination of two original units located on the 18th floor of a premier 1957 modernist lift slab building designed by architect Milton Schwartz, has views in all four directions, truly a spectacular residence that its owners wished to revitalize as their home plus offices, guest room area for family visitors, and space for a fitness center. The architects recommended a long parabolic wall to divide the space that conveys the visitor from entry to sitting areas, dining, kitchen, study areas, and bedrooms, while integrating very strict and specific functional and storage requirements. Architectural lighting was accomplished by the creation of soffits with light coves, carefully placed around the core. Thus, the ceiling plane affords a soft glow in each of the primary spaces. Maple flooring, white walls, and a few accented paint tones provide a crisp clear background for the couple's collection of 1940's and 1950's classic modern furniture. Regardless of view, the revamped residence provides high drama in an atypical manner for owners and guests alike.

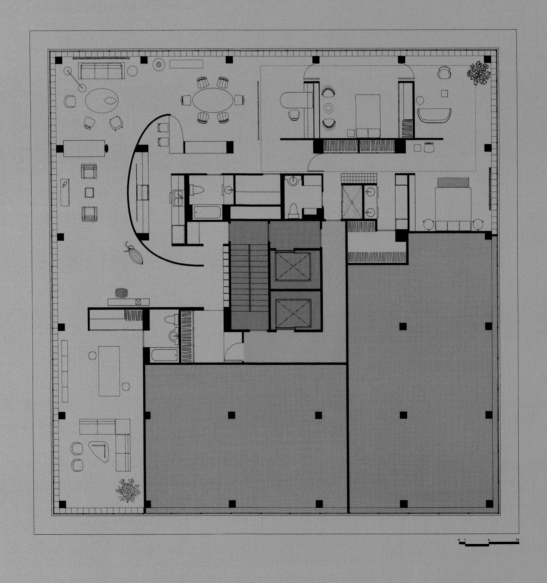

Paul Stuart Chicago, Men's Retail Clothing Store
Chicago, 1995

Occupying 27,000 square feet in the landmark John Hancock Center, this store, owned and operated by a prominent New York retailer, was designed to convey the sensibilities of the merchant and product. This was accomplished while taking advantage of a unique location.

The enclosed first floor embraces the customer with elegance. Flexible modular display walls of English brown oak provide backdrops for display, while concealing sophisticated lighting, on a floor plane of limestone and the store's signature bronze-gold wool carpet. The environment exudes the grace of an English gentleman's club with a modern vision. Customers are encouraged, by a dramatic spiral stair, to ascend to the second floor, offering a large array of menswear.

The vast second floor has been modulated into a gracious and comfortable set of sales rooms, giving definition and emphasis to various product lines. Unique modular cases allow for flexible displays and views out to the city, making an ever-changing store atmosphere. The greatest challenge was to transform the building lobby and elevator lobby spaces to functional working retail spaces.

Successfully conveying the updated classic style and high quality of the merchandise, this store has also been presented the "DesignWise" award by the Illinois chapter of the American Society of Interior Designers and awarded the "Grand Prize" by the National Association of Store Fixture Manufacturers.

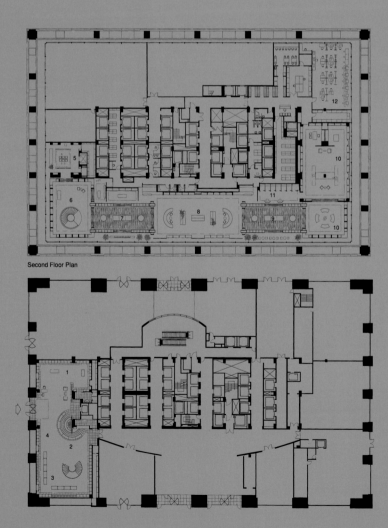

Second Floor Plan

Custom Furniture Designs

VANDERBILT GULFSIDE
APARTMENT COCKTAIL
TABLE W/SHELL COLLECTION

CHICAGO MERCANTILE EXCHANGE
EXHIBIT CASES

P/K OFFICE 645 NORTH MICHIGAN
BUILT-IN-RECEPTION SEATING

FIRST NATIONAL BANK
DINING TABLE AND WALL
HUNG CREDENZA

860 LAKESHORE DRIVE
APARTMENT, WOOD DINING
TABLE AND CHAIRS

LASALLE PARTNERS II
LEATHER WALL HUNG CREDENZA

LaSalle Partners Limited, Corporate Headquarters II
Chicago, 1996

This major real estate services company, having outgrown its fourteen-year-old headquarters, returned to Powell/Kleinschmidt for the design of a new facility that would bring them into the next century. The result is an environment of venerability and substance that seamlessly integrates technology, provides for expansion, and allows for frequent internal reorganization. Achieved within a strict budget, this innovative new corporate environment creates a new standard in office design.

Workstations were completely reconfigured to accommodate a multitude of tasks and individual staff requirements. Flexibility was provided so that with simple mechanical adjustments, swiftly made, staff can be reassigned with no disruption to the flow of work. In addition, all workstations are composed of a minimum number of parts, thus easing maintenance, simplifying purchasing, and reducing costs. The most ergonomic task chair, staff-tested and unanimously approved, is used throughout.

Rich hues of the same color give distinction and identity to each of the four floors, while work areas are open to dramatic exterior views and sunlight, creating an invigorating work environment. Sophisticated lighting works with the ceiling shapes to eliminate glare on computer screens, thus adding spacial dimension to work areas.

Complementing the open office area is a sophisticated conference center that brings together a boardroom, conference rooms, catering facilities, and the main reception lobby. Each meeting room integrates the state-of-the-art audio-visual and computer presentation equipment used to enhance all activities involving sales, marketing, and client outreach.

At the conclusion of the project, the client expressed complete satisfaction that the goals were fully met as well as genuine pride in the newly-designed spaces, where all employees can work and communicate effectively.

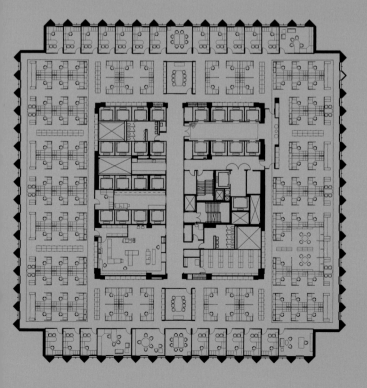 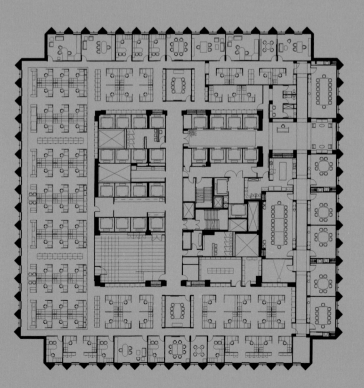

Kenneth Dayton Residence II
Minneapolis, Minnesota, 1997

When these former clients decided to move from their country house on a lake to a new home in the city, they deliberately chose to retain cherished furnishings designed by Powell/Kleinschmidt from their previous residence.

Hence, all layouts were drawn to accommodate their desires. A few new items of furniture were custom designed to solve specific functional problems. Also, their extensive art collection was judiciously culled keeping those works of art that retain the integrity of the collection and that give meaning to the everyday life of the owners.

Residence
Jupiter, Florida, 1998

The owners of this 9,000-square-foot home, located on a prime location facing the intercoastal waterway in Florida, wished to reorder the entire structure, incorporating principles of modernism and regionalism, and focusing on the natural elements of light, air, and water. The existing entry was transformed; in addition, a screened-in porch at the opposite end of the house was demolished and the entire rear elevation replaced with a double-height window wall, an open limestone terrace, and a new double-helix pool. The first floor was rebuilt as an open sweep of space with a newly added curving stairway that leads to the rebuilt balcony and library. A triangulated wood slat ceiling between beams further establishes a strong geometric order. A semicircular kitchen on the ground floor divides the service zone from the public spaces, while on the second level, the construction of a new master suite and guest quarters extends the architectural exercise.

Throughout the project, the material palette placed emphasis on neutrals in the stonework, pale woods, and textured plaster in wet beach-sand tones. Limestone pavers in 20-inch squares unify the entire floor plane. The lighting design furthers the goal of strengthening and illuminating key architectural elements and functionally responding to the program. Finally, the owners' superb art collection, acquired over the years, was skillfully placed throughout the home, each piece carefully lit by recessed sources concentrated at the perimeter. This assignment can be cited for its effective interplay between client and architect, producing a residence completely regional and, at the same time, very personal, reflecting the highest level of taste and refinement.

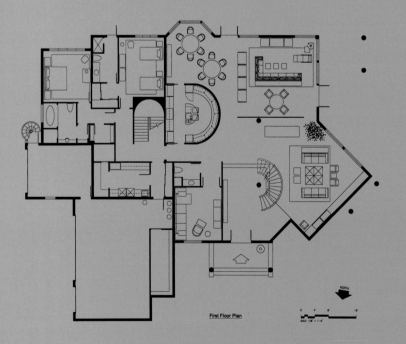

First Floor Plan

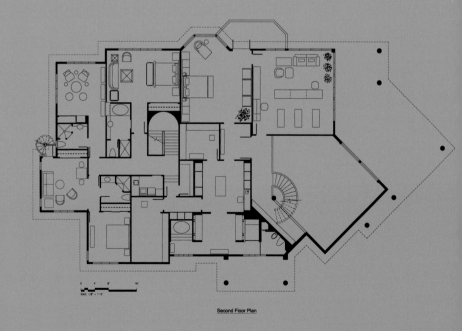

Second Floor Plan

Noble Associates Offices
Chicago, 1996

In addition to providing programming and design services, Powell/Kleinschmidt assisted Noble Associates in the search for space in Chicago which would establish the firm as a unique presence in the world of food product testing and advertising. The location chosen, a two-story space at the top of the distinguished Kenzo Tange designed A.M.A. building, has done just that.

The chambered nautilus – as a corporate symbol, with its subtle balance, unique form and interrelated parts – was used as a metaphor for planning this office environment. The workings of the organization are based on just the right balance of each interdependent department. The resultant open design allows divisions to work creatively and cooperatively. The dramatic two-story work space allowed for a balcony, which adds fifty percent more floor area at no extra rental cost. From this vantage point, creativity and communication flow from the test kitchen in which new products are developed, tested and presented to copywriters, then to marketers, and on to the client.

The Art Institute of Chicago, Restaurant on the Park
Chicago, 1999

This assignment involved the renovation of the Restaurant on the Park, the Art Institute of Chicago's premier dining area. Through the skillful introduction of more contemporary architecture in this twenty-four-year-old space, diners now enjoy more expansive vistas of the Grant Park scene from an uninterrupted wall of windows. The entirely renovated interior creates a mood of brightness and airiness with the soaring ceiling planes, all new furnishings, and complementary tabletop designs, enhanced by historic architectural fragments taken from the Art Institute's illustrious collection. A custom designed carpet inspired by a cross-hatch motif in a Jasper Johns painting provides a practical solution for floor covering. To fulfill specific functional needs, Powell/Kleinschmidt designed many of the one of a kind furniture items that include maitre d'station, cashier enclosure, bus service stations, special dessert table, reception area benches and occasional tables. Interweaving scenes of Chicago architecture and Midwest color, the transformation is a warm inviting and artistically enriching space, ensuring a notable dining experience.

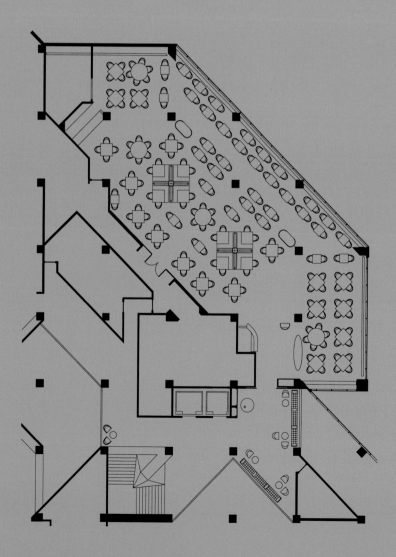

Art in Architecture

ROBERT STACKHOUSE
SCULPTURE PRUDENTIAL
NORTH CENTRAL
PLYMOUTH OPERATIONS

SHEILLA HICKS WALL HANGINGS
ONE MAIN PLACE LOBBY

GEORGE MORRISON REDWOOD
TOTEM, PRUDENTIAL NORTH
CENTRAL PLYMOUTH OPERATIONS

ARP SCULPTURE, SAM FRANCIS
PAINTING, FARLEY FOYER

DUBUFFET SCROLL
ONE MAGNIFICENT MILE
APARTMENT, MASTER BEDROOM

MITCHELL PAINTING, PEPPER
SCULPTURE, OLETSKI PAINTING,
CALDER SCULPTURE,
MOORE SCULPTURE,
FARLEY, LIVING ROOM

M. G. Rose Apartment
Chicago, 1999

From high above the city on the 58th floor, this client wished to create a home that would be a skillful blend of classic modern furniture, European antiques, African artifacts, and contemporary sculpture. Custom designed elements include a lacquered double door wine cooler at the end of the gallery corridor, various tables, a wall-hung stone foyer shelf and powder room including a rounded rosewood and onyx lavatory. The result, as these photographs amply document, is at once idiosyncratic and serene. The dramatic highlight of the 3,000-square-foot apartment is the corner living room that rises two floors in height with a stunning south and east view of Chicago's downtown and lakefront. Custom built-in seating along the south window composed of channeled suede cushions increases comfort and enhances the view.

Briarwood Country Club
Deerfield, Illinois, 2000

It is a truism that successful commissions are the consequence of respectful collaboration between client and the interior architecture firm retained by the client. So it is with the Briarwood Country Club, a suburban club facility wishing to renovate its three main rooms in the principal building. The client established project goals of refurbishment based on comfort and elegance, flexibility in serving differing event requirements, and strict adherence to an established budget and schedule. Powell/Kleinschmidt reclaimed such strong architectural features as the large circular living room fireplace and skylight, coating the dark bricks with a smooth skin of light plaster. The mirrors in the dining room ceiling coves were replaced by simple elegant metal mesh that reflects color throughout the spaces. Woven wood panels, mounted on casters, allow for easy adjustment in dining room and living room sizes, while colors and materials were selected in warm gray neutrals and wheat tones to maximize the view and visibility of the grounds for all club members and their guests. Every goal was fully met, an exemplary tribute to all the participants.

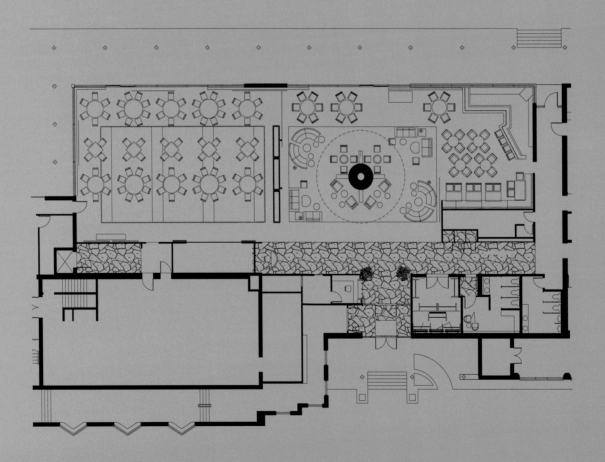

Cummins Residence, Renovation
Evanston, Illinois, 2001

This one-story town house, designed in the classic Miesian tradition and constructed by a Miesian disciple, David Haid, and then occupied by this talented architect, was sold following his death to a young couple with a great appreciation of the style and respect for the meticulous craftsmanship. They were enchanted with the punctuation of the enclosing brick walls by large glass openings that reveal court gardens. They stipulated a program of renovation of the foyer, living and dining areas, and new recessed lighting to emphasize the architecture and their significant Naïve Art collection. Furnishings consist of custom designed millwork and classic Mies furniture juxtaposed with a Jean Michel Frank sofa, three Italian-style lounge chairs and a rare tribal rug.

Ravinia Festival
Freehling Dining Room, Highland Park, Illinois, 1999

To expand the delight of outdoor summertime concerts of the Chicago Symphony Orchestra, many patrons frequently enjoy a pre-concert meal in the Freehling Dining Room, an early arts and crafts building in need of renovation and upgrade. This work focused on three specific areas: the foyer, the dining room, and the dining garden. A new octagonal window was added in stained glass, while new carpeting, a fresh paint scheme, re-upholstered dining chairs, table linens, table top accessories, and a fully landscaped garden now enhance the dining experience. Special lighting was developed to backlight the remaining clerestory windows utilized as art pieces placed on perimeter walls. The result effectively adds to the special quality of this dining room.

Cowtan & Tout Showrooms
Chicago, New York, San Francisco, 1999–2001

When Cowtan & Tout, a London-based fabric company, acquired space in Chicago's Merchandise Mart, it stipulated display settings that would dramatize its distinctive lines of both traditional and contemporary textiles. For maximum impact, the fabrics demand full-length display capability with complimentary lighting that enables the viewer to see the true look of every color and hue of these unique fabrics. The hardness of a wood plank floor contrasts with the softness of fabrics.

The new plan consists of two primary circulation axes that divide the showroom into distinct areas for each product line, with focal points that direct the flow of clients throughout all the spaces. Special lighting using both fluorescent and incandescent sources was used to achieve the effect of natural sunlight on all display walls and wings. Not only was Powell/Kleinschmidt's design scheme fully responsive to all the clients needs, the project was completed within the required 8-week schedule.

Following the completion of the Chicago commission, the owner awarded Powell/Kleinschmidt the renovation of its New York, and San Francisco showrooms.

Chicago

New York   San Francisco

Work in Progress
Apartment
Highland Park, Illinois, 2001

This apartment, designed as a summer residence, is a combination of two units, located in the center of a north suburban Chicago area. This work is a second commission for Powell/Kleinschmidt by a long-time client. The plan is organized around a long gallery corridor that links primary and secondary rooms and represents one of the firm's most minimally designed creations.

The corridor, living and dining areas, and family room all have special wall treatments designed to unify the space, while the secondary areas share multiple functions to replicate amenities customarily associated with an individual residence. The goals of the materials palette were several: to appear totally regional in look and feel to reflect a strong Midwest character; deliberately different from the same family's Jupiter, Florida residence by the incorporation of cooler neutral tonalities. Materials investigation has included using traditional materials in new ways. The search for new materials, stainless steel mesh, metallic lacquer, design of special carpets and implementation of new fabrics play a special note on the floor of 6-inch-wide, dark-brown oak-planks. The owners' love of 20th century art is reflected in the careful assembly of paintings and sculptures in each room.

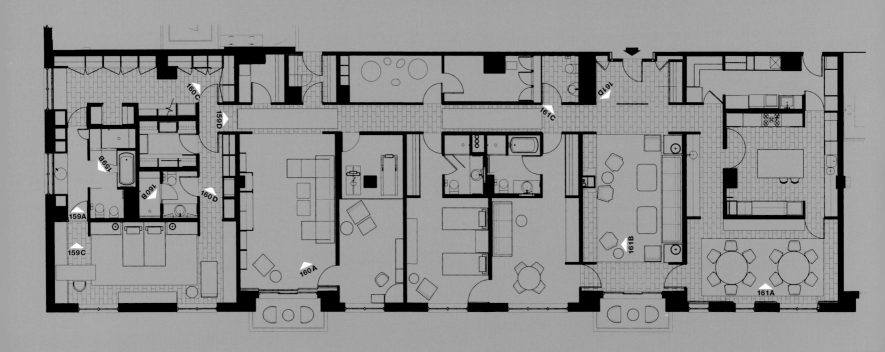

A

C

D

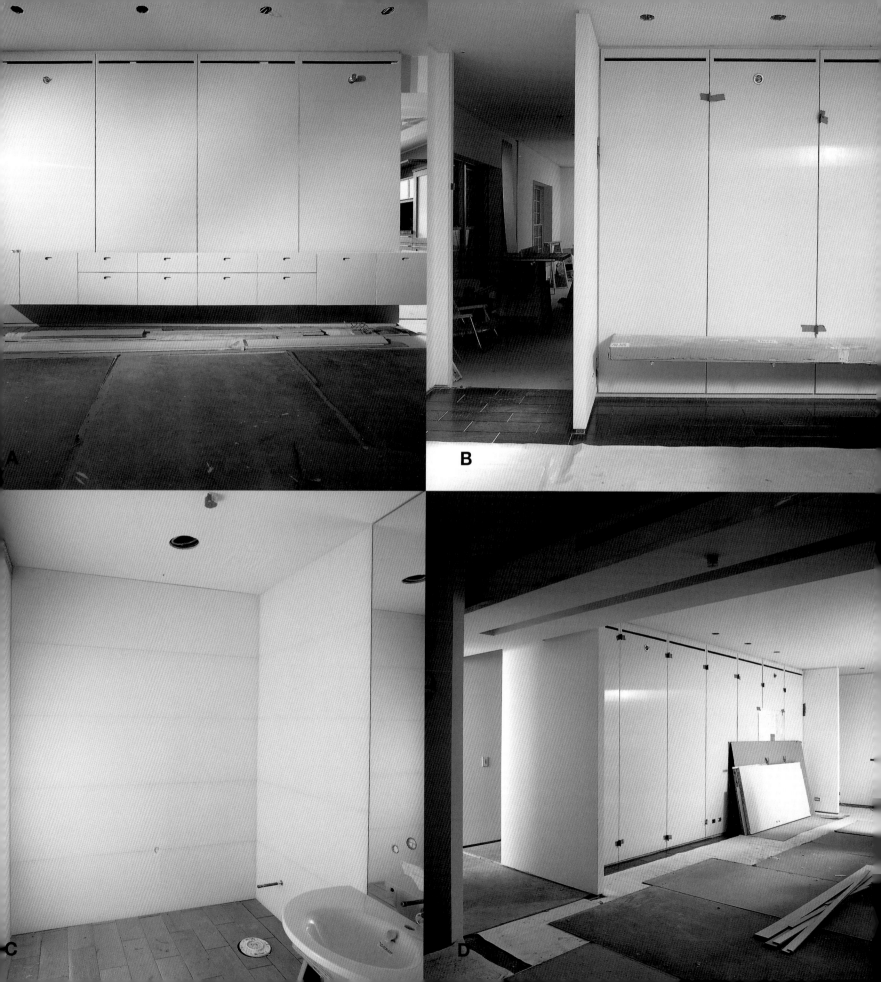

Work in Progress
Lobby Renovation
645 N. Michigan Avenue, Chicago

New property ownership is often accompanied by an objective appraisal as to a structure's appearance. In the case of the 645 North Michigan Avenue lobby, the new owners' first order of business was to provide life and vitality to the tired entry of their prestigious building advantageously located in the heart of Chicago's premier shopping area. Powell/Kleinschmidt's response to the assignment includes: new flame cut black granite flooring from the exterior curb directly to the building elevators; a glass-roofed canopy that allows for maximum light penetration; a new revolving door; lobby-side walls of frosted white glass; back-lite to increase the source of light; rosewood paneling for the elevator core; and a seven-foot-high tapestry to provide an art component for the lobby. Throughout the plan, supreme care has been taken to maintain the integrity of the base building design. The new owners have high expectations for this program of upgrade and refurbishment.

Work in Progress
Chicago Board Options Exchange, Chicago

The Chicago Board Options Exchange, the renowned trading facility dealing in options, engaged Powell/Kleinschmidt to design new general offices in a building adjacent to their parent offices to include enclosed and open offices, conference rooms, kitchen, and support areas needed for an efficient business operation. Primary emphasis concerns the provision of effective illumination for both the enclosed and open offices. In addition to a fresh, innovative space plan, Powell/Kleinschmidt is developing a completely new colors-and-materials palette reflective of the Midwestern light and appropriate for the new spaces.

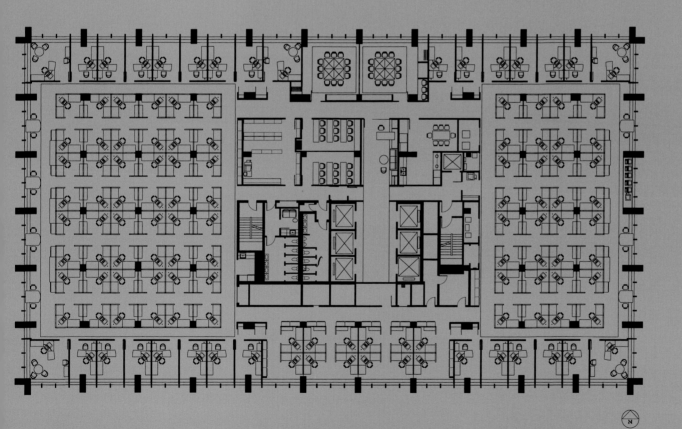

Work in Progress
Harris Beach Law Offices
Rochester, New York, 2001

When one of New York state's largest law firms relocated from an urban high-rise building to a suburban 70's building built in the brutalist style of the time, it presented Powell/Kleinschmidt with a unique challenge.
The building, although situated in a campus setting with spectacular landscape views, was limited by the amount of window perimeter available for private office use.
P/K responded to the challenge by proposing an additional interior atrium providing both additional windows and a two-story reading room for the Library on the first floor. Additionally, the perimeter use was maximized by limiting all office widths to 10 feet and varying the office depth. Creating glass fronts on all the perimeter offices and providing clerestories where possible maximized exterior light penetration and make daylight available to the entire staff. This, accompanied by the careful use of indirect lighting solutions, created the quality of light appropriate to the building site and compatible with the computer-intensive environment required for a law firm. The offices for attorneys are arranged according to practice and in neighborhood suites between the atriums and building perimeter. A cafeteria space that may alternately be reconfigured for assembly is also being planned. Completion is anticipated for August, 2001.

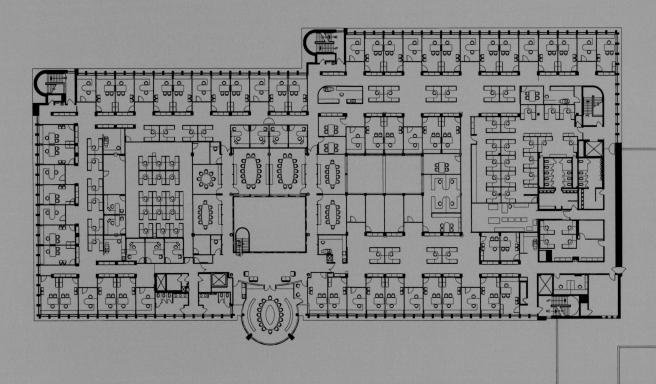

Acknowledgements

It is impossible to thank adequately the hundreds of people who have made this book possible, beginning with those who worked initially on each project during the course of our quarter-century existence and ending with the development and editing of this publication. Mindful of the advice of a notable historian who cautioned about curbing the tendency to reel off fulsome acknowledgements for every paper clip we borrow during the course of preparing a manuscript, nonetheless, we wish to acknowledge our deepest gratitude to those people who have been important to us.

During our early association with Skidmore, Owings & Merrill, we worked with and gained inspiration from insightful colleagues who set high standards for architectural excellence. We were privileged to be part of Walter A. Netsch's studio. His gifts and talents have shaped our outlook on architecture and art to this day. Later, we moved to the studio of Bruce Graham, a master in dealing with large corporate clients and developers, whose strong design principles and relentless commitment to quality remain inspirational. When we established our firm and were searching for suitable location, Harry Weese generously offered us space in his offices; and Pete and Lawrence Zake of Lakeside Furniture taught us the basics of Upholstery 101 and encouraged us to build our firm. The entire Hedrich Blessing organization has endlessly assisted during the past 25 years in photographically conveying our spaces and their intricate details to the world.

We owe a lasting debt to those clients who have stimulated us to produce unimagined results and who have rejoiced in our accomplishments. Similarly, colleagues in other firms and related fields have encouraged us to develop fresh design solutions, incorporating new technologies to improve the environment in which people live and work.

The publication of this volume also permits us to pay tribute to our office colleagues. Many have been with Powell/Kleinschmidt for many years encouraging their newer associates, taking pride in past achievements as well as sharing in the burdens of disappointment and frustration that inevitably occur. We are deeply indebted to Dorothy Ver Steeg, a long-time associate and friend, whose role as "Director of Special Projects" has covered assignments too numerous to list. She has been responsible for all the text in this volume. We also want to acknowledge the advice and counsel of our Board of Directors.

Finally, it is with special gratitude that we cite the skilled editorial and graphic design contributions of Werner Blaser, Ernst Sturm and also the role of Birkhäuser – Publishers for Architecture. Without their help, this volume, long dreamed of and hoped for, simply would not have been possible.

Donald D. Powell
Robert D. Kleinschmidt

Above: (Left to right)
Shannon Banks, Daniel Moore, Patricia Natzke, John Padmore, Laureen Axelrod.
Row 2: William Arnold, Charlie Cunov, Donna Edwards, Beth Nilsson, Donald Los,
Jennifer Miller, Donald Powell, Ursula Dayenian, Robert Kleinschmidt.
At Right: (Front to back)
Kimberly Maurer, Juana Maria Fittip, Thomas Roeman

William E. Arnold

Since joining Powell/Kleinschmidt in 1983, Mr. Arnold has planned over a million square feet of law offices as well as completing a variety of retail, hospitality, and residential projects. Of particular interest to Mr. Arnold is the quality of light and the role it plays in the expression of interior architecture. He holds a Bachelors of Design Degree from the University of Cincinnati.

Charles Robert Cunov

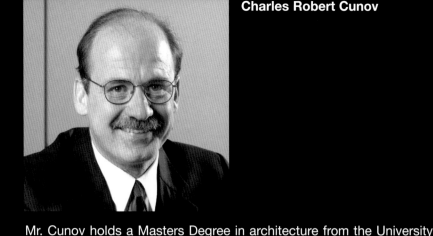

Mr. Cunov holds a Masters Degree in architecture from the University of Michigan and joined Powell/Kleinschmidt in 1984. His responsibilities have evolved from planning through project management including an overall perspective and coordination of Powell/Kleinschmidt projects through his role as Director of Projects. In 2000, Mr. Cunov, a licensed architect, was named managing agent for the practice of architecture at Powell/Kleinschmidt and serves on the Board of Directors.

Thomas Lambert Boeman

Mr. Boeman has been a member of the staff of Powell/Kleinschmidt since receiving his Bachelors Degree in architecture from the University of Cincinnati in 1987. His project responsibilities include planning and architectural design for a variety of project types. As a principal of the firm, Mr. Boeman has been active and instrumental in the development of the computer based tools used by Powell/Kleinschmidt in the design and production of their projects. A licensed architect, Mr. Boeman was named to the Board of Directors of Powell/Kleinschmidt in 2000.

Donna Jean Edwards

Ms. Edwards has been with Powell/Kleinschmidt since 1988 after receiving her Bachelors Degree in Interior Design from Harrington Institute of Interior Design. She is currently a principal at Powell/Kleinschmidt whose primary roles include design, project management, and office management. Ms. Edwards also serves on the Powell/Kleinschmidt Board of Directors.

Donald Los

Mr. Los attended the Illinois Institute of Technology and The School of the Art Institute of Chicago and has been with Powell/Kleinschmidt Inc. since 1985. He is currently a principal at Powell/Kleinschmidt Inc. with responsibilities including project management, coordination of construction technologies, and implementation of CAD drafting standards.

Acord, Gary
Adams, Leah
Arms, David
* Arnold, William
Axelrod, Laureen
Baehr, Jay
Banks, Shannon
Baughmann-Sauder, Cheryl
Bebart, Barry
Behm, Victoria
Bell, Patricia
Berlinghof, Emily
Bjorling, Linnea
Bodenstein, Leslie
* Boeman, Thomas
Briggins, Danielle
Burdi, Beth
Cataldo, Robert
Crawford, J. Ronald
* Cunov, Charles
Davidson, Ronald
Dayenian, Ursula
Demierre, Stacey
Duffy, Colleen
* Edwards, Donna
Esposito, Patrick
Fisher, Mark
Fittin, Juana Maria
Fletcher, Mary
Goddard, Debra
Grasmehr, Mark
Graue, David
Harris, Hayley
Heistand, Yvonne
Huchting, William
Kelly, Sarah

Leady, Robert
Lesinsky, Michael
Liddell, Charolette
* Los, Donald
Maurer, Kimberly
McCarthy, John
McConnell, Patrick
Miller, Jennifer
Miller, Sandra
Million, Michael
Moore, Daniel
Nanna, Susan
Natzke, Patricia
Nelson, Mark
Nelson, Zora
Nilsson, Beth
Padmore, John
Patterson, Gregory
Piotrowski, Robert
Robertson, Tiana
Rule, Charlene
Sakai, Yoko
Schneider, Jim
Slater, Kenneth
Steele, David
Steigert, Jim
Thomas, David
Titterton, George
Tousey, Steven
Twiss, Richard
Van Mell, Sandy
Ver Steeg, Dorothy
Vrba, Mark
Walega, Doug
Walt, Brandon
Wipachit, Apinya

Future of the Firm

The publication of this volume, documenting and celebrating a quarter century of interior architectural accomplishments, affords an opportunity to look to the future. Five recently appointed principals – William Arnold, Thomas Boeman, Charles Cunov, Donna Edwards, Donald Los – and other talented staff members ensure continuity and adherence to the high standards for which Powell/Kleinschmidt is universally recognized, as well as the promise of even greater achievements in the future. The firm anticipates continuing close ties to clients from past projects, advancing works currently in progress, and meeting the needs and challenges of future clients.

Total Works 1976–2001

Year	Project	City, State
1976	Powell/Kleinschmidt Inc.	Chicago
	Van Meter Residence	Springfield, IL
	Kogut Residence	Evanston, IL
	Harris Bank Remote Facility	Chicago
1977	Gretchen Bellinger Inc. Showroom	New York
	Kenneth Bellinger Residence	Sea Island, GA
	Northwestern University Graduate School Administration	Evanston, IL
1978	The Prudential Insurance Company of America	Merrillville, IN
	Gretchen Bellinger Inc., Executive Offices and Warehouse	New York
	Knoll International Showroom	Chicago
	Nancy Hoffman Apartment	New York
	Illinois Housing Development Authority	Chicago
1979	Gretchen Bellinger Inc. Showroom, Remodeling	New York
	Broadwell's Drug Store	Springfield, IL
	American Steel Foundries	Chicago
	GF Showroom	Chicago
	The Prudential Mid-America Home Office	Chicago
	Interior Crafts Showroom	Chicago
1980	Vanderbilt Gulfside Apartment	Naples, FL
	Newberger Apartment	Chicago
	Cicero Residence	Evanston, IL
1981	The Bates Apartment	Chicago
	The Prudential Insurance Company of America	Plymouth, MN
1982	One Magnificent Mile Apartment	Chicago
	One Magnificent Mile Lobby Renovation	Chicago
	The Prudential Real Estate Division	Chicago
	Illinois Masonic Hospital Barr Pavilion Cafeteria	Chicago
	Illinois Masonic Hospital West Entry Gardens	Chicago
1983	LaSalle Partners Limited, Corporate Headquarters I	Chicago
	Gretchen Bellinger Apartment	New York
	Chicago Bar Association	Chicago
	Gustafson Residence	Bel-Air, FL
1984	Northwestern University Law School	Chicago
	The Wrigley Building Lobbies	Chicago
	Merchandise Mart Conference Center and Executive Offices	Chicago
1985	Steelcase/Stow & Davis Showroom	Atlanta, GA
	860 Lake Shore Drive Apartment	Chicago
	Hopkins & Sutter Law Offices	Chicago
	Pattishall, McAuliffe & Hofstetter Law Offices	Chicago
	Merrill Lynch Investment Offices	Appleton, WI
1986	Powell/Kleinschmidt Offices 645 N. Michigan Ave.	Chicago
	One Main Place, Lobby Renovation	Dallas, TX
	Farley Apartment	Chicago
	Merrill Lynch Investment Offices	Lansing, MI
	Merrill Lynch Investment Offices	Rockford, IL
	Merrill Lynch Regional Offices, Sears Tower	Chicago
1987	Chicago Mercantile Exchange, Executive Offices	Chicago
	Dickinson, Wright, Moon, Vandusen & Freeman Law Offices	Detroit, MI
	Dykema Gossett Conference Center	Detroit, MI
	Merrill Lynch Investment Offices	Oak Brook, IL

1988	Mayer, Brown & Platt Law Offices	Chicago
	SunarHauserman Furniture Collection	Cleveland, OH
	The Standard Club Renovations	Chicago
1989	Kenneth Dayton Residence I	Wayzata, MN
	Woodwork Corporation of America, Executive & Administrative Offices	Chicago
	Scott Miller Apartments I & II	Chicago
	880 Lake Shore Drive Residence	Chicago
	First National Bank of Chicago, Executive Dining 57th Floor	Chicago
1990	Illinois Institute of Technology, Kent College of Law	Chicago
	Grippo & Elden Law Offices	Chicago
	Vector Securities Offices	Northbrook, IL
	Simmons Residence	Chicago
1991	University of Chicago Graduate School of Business	Chicago
	Naperville City Hall	Naperville, IL
	The RREEF Funds Corporate Headquarters	Chicago
	Wolpert Residence	Chicago
	330-340 West Diversey Apartments Lobby and Corridors Renovation	Chicago
1992	GATX Corporation, Corporate Headquarters	Chicago
	Green Acres Country Club	Northbrook, IL
	Fruit of the Loom Corporate Aircraft I	Chicago
	Ryan-Kralovec Penthouse	Chicago
	Kennelly Square Condominiums, Common Areas	Chicago
	1350–1360 N. Lake Shore Drive Common Areas, Lobbies, Corridors	Chicago
1993	Merrill Lynch Investment Offices	Chicago
	Kreuger International, Furniture Systems, File Systems	Chicago
	The Art Institute of Chicago Museum Shop	Chicago
1994	John D. & Catherine T. MacArthur Foundation	Chicago
	Rooks, Pitts & Poust Law Offices	Chicago
	Pickleman Apartment	Chicago
	Mahoney Hawks & Goldings Law Offices	Boston, MA
	Morris Residence	Northbrook, IL
	Friedland Residence	Jupiter, FL
1995	Paul Stuart, Men's Retail Clothing Store	Chicago
	Olympia Center Condominium Lobby	Chicago
	Ryan-Kralovec Pavilion	Saugatuck, MI
	161 E. Chicago Lobby	Chicago
	990 Lake Shore Drive Condominium Corridors	Chicago
	645 N. Michigan Ave. Lobby	Chicago
	Francis W. Parker School Phase I, II, III, IV	Chicago
	Art Institute of Chicago Museum Shop	Chicago
	Cyrus Lowe Apartment	New York
	Lowe Apartment	New York
1996	Noble Associates Offices	Chicago
	LaSalle Partners Limited, Corporate Headquarters II	Chicago
	The Chicagoan	Chicago
	Fruit of the Loom Corporate Aircraft II	Chicago
	Frontenac Corporate Offices	Chicago
	Hines – 225 Wacker Lobby Renovation	Chicago
	Hines – Three First National Plaza Lobby, Corridors Renovation	Chicago
	Hines – Three First National Plaza Reception Room	Chicago
	Hines – 5215 Old Orchard Lobby, Corridor Renovation	Skokie, IL
	Hines-Huntington Center	Columbus, OH
	Kennelly Square Apartments, Common Areas	Chicago
	Mayer, Brown & Platt	Chicago

1997	Kenneth Dayton Residence II	Minneapolis, MN
	The Birchwood Club	Highland Park, IL
	Morant Residence	Chicago
	Sony Michigan Avenue Refurbishment	Chicago
1998	Fixler Residence	Jupiter, FL
	Cowtan & Tout Showroom	Chicago
	Lowe Apartment	Seattle, WA
	Museum of Science & Industry Executive Dining Room	Chicago
	Olympia Fields Country Club	Olympia Fields, IL
	Birchwood Country Club	Highland Park, IL
	Harvey Krane Residence	Chicago
	Hines – 225 Wacker	Chicago
	Hines – Chiquita Center Lobby	Cincinnatti, OH
	Hines Interests Lobby Renovation	Schaumburg, IL
	Judd Enterprises	Chicago
	LaSalle Partners Expansion	Chicago
	Chicago Housing Authority Unit Offices	Chicago
	College of DuPage, Fine Arts Center Lobby	Glen Ellyn, IL
	Domoras Residence	Chicago
	Kenneth Fixler Residence	Northbrook, IL
	Graunke Residence	Barrington, IL
	Graunke Kicakpoo Farms	Barrington, IL
	Grippo & Elden	Chicago
	Halvorsen & Kaye Engineering Offices	Chicago
	Mallul Apartment	Chicago
	Terrence Dowd Residence	Glenview, IL
	Ver Steeg Residence	Lake Forest, IL
	Segal Residence	Winnetka, IL
1999	Art Institute of Chicago, Restaurant on the Park	Chicago
	Freehling Room Ravinia Festival	Highland Park, IL
	M.G. Rose Apartment	Chicago
	Wells Residence	Deerfield, IL
	Briarwood Country Club	Chicago
2000	Bang & Olufsen America	Schaumburg, IL
	Chicago Board Options Exchange Office Renovation	Chicago
	Christ Apartment	Chicago
	Park Millennium Lobby and all Common Areas	Chicago
	Cowtan & Tout Showroom	Chicago
	Cowtan & Tout Showroom	San Francisco, CA
	Cowtan & Tout Showroom	New York
	Fasano Residence	Chicago
	Hines – Woodfield Corporate Center, Public Areas	Schaumburg, IL
	Howe Barnes Expansion	Chicago
	Mohn Residence	Woodfield, IL
	Robert Morris College	Chicago
	RREEF Expansion 2000	Chicago
	Simmons Residence, Renovation	Chicago
	United Airlines, Flight Attendant Domicile Facilities	O'Hare, Boston, Denver, Las Vegas
2001	Cummins Residence, Renovation	Evanston, IL
	Fixler Apartment	Highland Park, IL
	Harris Beach Law Offices	Rochester, NY
	Perry Penthouse	Chicago

Photographic Credits

Hedrich Blessing
11 West Illinois Street
Chicago, IL 60610

Jim Hedrich	9, 17, 21, 23, 24, 25, 26, 27, 28, 33, 37, 38, 39, 40, 41, 122, 144
Nick Merrick	43
Jon Miller	44, 46, 47, 48, 49, 53, 54, 55, 56, 57, 59, 60, 61, 63, 64, 65, 66, 67, 75, 76, 77, 79, 81, 82, 83, 85, 86, 87, 88, 89, 91, 92, 95, 96, 97, 101, 102, 103, 104, 105, 107, 108, 109, 111, 117, 118, 119, 120, 121, 122, 123, 126, 127, 128
Christopher Barrett	6, 7, 124, 129, 133, 134, 135, 136, 137, 140, 142, 143, 146, 147, 149, 150, 151, 152, 153, 154, 155, 158, 159, 160, 161

Don DuBroff Photography	78, 115, 138, 139, 145
500 Riverwood Road	
Charlotte, NC 28270	

Esto Photographics Inc
222 Valley Place
Mamaroneck, NY 10543

Ezra Stoller	116
David Franzen	19, 97

Charlie Mayer Photography	113
819 W. Washington	
Oak Park, IL 60302	

Peter Paige	51
7 Sunset Lane	
Upper Saddle River, NJ 07458	

Tony Soluri Photography	35, 156, 168, 169
1147 W. Ohio Street	
Chicago, IL 60622	

John Rodgers Photography	144
Dallas, TX	

Werner Blaser	46
Basel, Switzerland	

Don F. Wong	130, 131
8919 Vincent Place	
Bloomington, MN 55431	

Rendering Credits

Kevin Nield	162, 165
www.kevinnield.com	